It is hidden but always present

Lao-tzu

The Tao

Conversations on Chinese Art in Australia

Tianli Zu

Dr Tianli Zu is an Australian multimedia artist who was born in Beijing, China. For more information, please visit www.tianlizu.com.

The Tao: Conversations on Chinese Art in Australia
Copyright © 2018 by Tianli Zu. All rights reserved. No part of this book may be used or reproduced in any manner whatsoever without the written permission of the author except for brief quotations embodied in critical articles and reviews.

A record of this book is available from the National Library of Australia.

ISBN 978 1 72704 032 6

Front cover art and book design by Tianli Zu
Available from Amazon Books worldwide

Contents

Introduction	v
Chapter I: Innocence	1
Building people-to-people relationships Conversation with Jocelyn Chey	7
Resonating with traditional Chinese attitudes Conversation with Mae Anna Pang	35
'There is something going on over there …'	61
'Let's do it again!' Conversation with Edmund Capon	81
Chapter II: Hold on to the Centre	93
'I was really lucky in Australia' Conversation with Guan Wei	99
'The interesting part wasn't simply relating to art, it was relating to China itself' Conversation with Gene Sherman	115

A creative period that produced great artists 133
Conversation with Nicholas Jose

Is it possible to play? 155
Conversation with Liu Xiaoxian

'I choose to drift' 171
Conversation with Ah Xian

Chapter III: The Value of Adversity 193

'I came back!' 199
Conversation with Xiao Lu

'Our art is our world and our world is our experience' 213
Conversation with Wang Zhiyuan

'I ran away from Australia … to make art' 231
Conversation with Lin Chunyan

'Definitely contemporary Chinese art' 243
Conversation with Shen Shaomin

Chapter IV: Continuity 263

A very hands-on Chinese art curator 269
Conversation with Claire Roberts

'I am here all the time, observing it, taking it in and being part of it' 285
Conversation with Brian Wallace

Art broadens the relationship 301
Conversation with Geoff Raby

The roles that 4A played 315
Conversation with Aaron Seeto

'Suddenly difference becomes interesting, and 335
difference become attractive'
Conversation with John Yu

Acknowledgements 349

Glossary 351

Index 357

Introduction

This book is a series of conversations with people in Australia and China who contributed not only to cultural change but to social change. Art may not resolve social issues directly but by pursuing the same causes and interests, it can be used to attain understanding. The starting point was a conversation with Edmund Capon whose exhibition 'The First Chinese Emperor' showed at the Art Gallery of NSW and across Australia in 1982–83. Over one million Australians saw that exhibition but had no idea how it took shape. I was drawn immediately to this story. Not only had it never been documented in art history, but it also opened up a new way for Chinese people to recognise themselves from a Western perspective, and for Westerners to accept Chinese art and culture, while still appreciating the differences. Beginning in 2016 with Capon, this project expanded into a collection of dialogues that encompass cross-border artistic encounters.

Tao means the Way, the eternally unfolding and dynamic way of the universe. Chinese philosopher Lao-Tzu cultivated the Tao through his work, the *Tao Te Ching*. I employ the Tao in a practical way, as a means of pursuing balance through the interplay between polarities – yin and yang in Chinese terms – within space and time, the self and the other, east and west, past and present, negative and positive, implicit and explicit, dismembered and remembered, control and spontaneity.

These interplays are fundamental to the traditional and contemporary world.

The Tao: Conversations on Chinese Art in Australia looks behind the scenes of art exhibitions and the process of art making to reveal the way art resonates with society and to uncover interrelationships with politics, the economy and culture. It weaves its way through a narrative formed through dialogues with some influential people to explore attitudes, perceptions and emotions that elicit profound reflections on intertwining Eastern and Western mentalities in the context of Chinese art in Australia. It draws out cause and effect, and sheds light on interconnections between seemingly unrelated events. *The Tao: Conversations on Chinese Art in Australia* is a three-fold exploration between the present and the past, China and the West, and the individual and the collective.

In 1972, Australia and China established diplomatic relations and, along with this development, Chinese art was introduced to Australians, in many cases for the first time. Since then, contemporary Chinese art has mirrored the social changes, problems, and contradictions of the 45 years that followed. Its functionality has been evident from the very beginning of the Australian encounter with China. The curiosity and affection aroused by China through its art in Australia has never been overshadowed by political and economic changes.

What is Chinese art? In simple terms, Chinese art is a visual form, whether traditional or contemporary, distinguished by unique characteristics and aesthetics. China, with over 3000 years of recorded history to the present, attracts and holds world attention. One of the most obvious attractions is the greatness of Chinese art. The intention of this book is to give a sense of the way Chinese art interconnects and overlaps with Australia society. Chinese art is not static. It is not restricted by time or geographic location. As we see, it seizes the chance to extend its reach.

When the Chinese relics were exhibited in Australia, they provided new meanings for viewers to respond to and reflect on. Similarly, contemporary Chinese art reiterates the truth that has been spoken for thousands of years. In the early 1990s, Australian art museums exhibited art by contemporary Chinese artists, at a time when their works were not accepted in China. These dialogues are testimonies by those who shone a light, forming a kind of bridge that brought Chinese traditions into the contemporary world. Chinese art is consistent with Chinese philosophy and traditional thinking. Like all things in the universe, it is eternally changing and renewing itself.

The way I conducted conversations was intuitive and conscious control, and the dialogue acted like a two-way mirror. The conversations would have not developed if both sides had not engaged sincerely, with a shared respect for the significance of art. I researched the work and background of each person in depth before and after they agreed to talk to me. Then I spent an hour of face-to-face dialogue with each of them – inquiring, communicating, reflecting, and consulting spontaneously at the time and place of the conversation. I dictated the recorded conversations personally, and sent the text to each individual for clarification and confirmation.

In the conversations, I appear to be a shadow figure in the yin–yang interrelationship – either a follower seeking the views of the master, who respectfully responds, or to one side, challenging my interlocutor with questions that have more than one answer. *The Tao* reflects the spontaneous processes involved in changing societal attitudes. Through these dialogues with a range of influential people, the reader is transformed from a mere observer into one who engages in the conversation.

In addition to discussion and exchange of ideas, there is another dimension embedded in these conversations, and that is a dialogue I have with my inner world in order to connect with the outer world. I employ the *I Ching* divination process – the three-coin throwing method – to examine the hidden meaning, or the unsayable, from what has been said. I share some answers from the results of my coin-throwing to demonstrate the significance of this practice.

The Tao: Conversations on Chinese Art in Australia consists of four parts: Innocence; Hold on to the Centre; The Value of Adversity; and Continuity. This book adopts a circular methodology, in contrast to many other art history books which follow a chronological order. There is no beginning or end. The terminology makes use of dialectical and philosophical concepts to interpret connections.

Innocence appears in Chapter One because it presents three significant pioneers. Jocelyn Chey, the first cultural counsellor at the Australian Embassy in Beijing, took the first Australian landscape painting exhibition to Beijing in 1976. Mae Anna Pang, an Asian art curator at the National Gallery of Victoria, looks back on the first Chinese painting exhibition in Australia in 1981. Edmund Capon, long-time director of the Art Gallery of NSW with a deep knowledge of Chinese art and culture, organised the first Chinese

Emperor exhibition, 'Qin Shi Huang: Terracotta Warriors and Horses' for Australia in 1982–83, marking the tenth anniversary of Australia–China diplomatic relations. These people have tirelessly promoted Chinese art and built strong relationships between Australia and China from the 1970s until the present day.

Chapter Two, **Hold on to the Centre**, is a set of five conversations. Three are with contemporary Chinese-Australian artists, Guan Wei, Liu Xiaoxian and Ah Xian. Gene Sherman is a highly successful art dealer and gallery director. Hers was one of the first Australian galleries to show contemporary Chinese art. Nicholas Jose was cultural counsellor at the Australian Embassy in China during the traumatic time of the 1989 Tiananmen Massacre in Beijing. Jose played a crucial role supporting and promoting Chinese artists, helping them settle in and become successful in Australia. These dialogues explore profound friendships between Chinese artists and Australians as they recount how they made art a language of communication with Australians. The early 1990s was not only a turning point for some Chinese artists who came to Australia, but it also changed the way Australians see China today.

Conversation moves spontaneously but it has purpose. Chapter Three, **The Value of Adversity**, consists of dialogues with four artists, Xiao Lu, Wang Zhiyuan, Lin Chunyan and Shen Shaomin. Tracing these Chinese-Australian artists' paths reveals a fascinating commonality. They tried very hard to come to Australia, but didn't stay, instead returning to China around 2000 by choice. For the first time, these dialogues document the obstacles to creativity and development, and the limitations faced by Chinese artists in

Australia. While some artists continue to work in Australia, equally, many have returned to China to make art and to become successful in ways that Australia could not offer.

Chapter Four, **Continuity,** selects five conversations concerned with challenges Chinese art has encountered in Australia and how they were overcome. Claire Roberts curated 'New Art from China' (1992), the first contemporary Chinese art exhibition in an Australia art museum. Brian Wallace set up Red Gate Gallery, the first private gallery in Beijing, in 1991. Aaron Seeto talks about his time as the director of 4A Centre for Contemporary Asian Art, an artists' association founded in 1996. Geoff Raby, former Australian Ambassador to China and economist gives an account of promoting and collecting contemporary Chinese art. John Yu, Australian of the Year, employed art as a healing process in the New Children's Hospital at Westmead. These dialogues touch on how to place Chinese art in an Australia context, how to make the work speak to Australian viewers, and how to turn unfamiliar art forms and styles into part of the Australian experience. This chapter also investigates why this may not always be possible to achieve.

Throughout the book I have dialogued with individuals who shared their views based on personal experiences. I have discovered more about each person's perspective and understanding, although they fall under the same umbrella, that of Chinese art. In my view, it is not important how much a person understands about Chinese art, or whether the views are one sided. From these stories I have found that most people share the same view about the inseparable relationship between art and society. For Westerners, their affection for Chinese history, language and aesthetics is closely entwined with an interest in art. What intrigued me most was how to get them to open up and tell me about the hitherto untold stories of hard work behind the scenes. I offer readers their insights on Chinese art in Australia and hope that it will invite further conversations.

I must acknowledge that there is debate, argument, and conflict, too. And for those who spoke, inevitably their ideas and thoughts have evolved with time according the Tao, the ever-changing law of nature. These profound encounters with Chinese art in Australia offer readers an opportunity to reinterpret, reflect on and join in the dialogue. The Tao has begun …

Tianli Zu

Chapter I

The Tao gives birth to all beings,
nourishes them, maintains them,
cares for them, comforts them, protects them,
takes them back to itself,
creating without possessing,
acting without expecting,
guiding without interfering.

Lao-tzu, *Tao Te Ching*, Chapter 51

Innocence

The title of this chapter, Innocence, comes from my *I Ching* throws. It signifies simplicity, sincerity and the primal self.

The chapter contains three conversations with three distinguished scholars: Jocelyn Chey, Mae Anna Pang and Edmund Capon. In our conversations about introducing and promoting Chinese art in Australia in the early 1980s, they reflect on the concepts of nature and outlook on life. These ideas form the conceptual basis of the book.

I was seeking answers on two levels: first, the historical sequence and position of important events, and secondly, examining aspects that are not strictly historical events but which have come to assume broad cultural significance. For me, the accuracy of the accounts is not the most important issue. I take on all views, darting back and forth to inquire into the essence of Chinese art and its role in Australian culture. These dialogues with Capon, Pang and Chey opened up new interpretations that intrigued me and prompted deeper exploration.

In the first conversation Chey proposed 'building people-to-people relationships' as the first phase of the process. There is a progression from curiosity and interest in Chinese culture within a circle of friends until the second process takes over. For Pang, an essential aspect is to 'resonate with traditional Chinese attitudes'. Her interpretation incorporates a detailed study of Chinese history, philosophy, aesthetics and art. In the third conversation Capon combines instinct and research, spontaneous and non-spontaneous developments in his description of the discovery of the terracotta warriors. 'There is something going on over there …' gives a vivid account of how Chinese art attracted an Australian audience.

These three dialogues explore three discrete elements: the vitality of Chinese art, the perspective of nature, and the evolution of culture. Capon, Pang and Chey's collective thoughts – reflecting Western interpretations and refining the characteristics of Chinese art – were neither set up together initially, nor connected intentionally. These commonalities appeared purely by chance.

To deepen my understanding of the complementarity in the content of Chey, Pang and Capon had done, I asked the *I Ching* for an explanation of the main purpose of their actions. I found an answer in hexagram 25, *Wu Wang*, Innocence (The unexpected). Wilhelm translates it as:

ABOVE: THE CREATIVE, HEAVEN
BELOW: THE AROUSING, THUNDER

When, in accord with this, movement follows the law of heaven, man is innocent and without guile. His mind is natural and true, unshadowed by reflection or ulterior designs. For wherever conscious purpose is to be seen, there the truth and innocence of nature have been lost. Nature that is not directed by the spirit is not truth but degenerate nature. Starting out with the idea of the natural, the train of thought in part goes somewhat further and thus the hexagram includes also the idea of the fundamental or unexpected.

THE JUDGMENT
Innocence. Supreme success.
Perseverance furthers.
If someone is not he should be,
He has misfortune,

And it does not further him
To undertake anything.

By devotion to this divine spirit within himself, he attains an unsullied innocence that leads him to do right with instinctive sureness and without any ulterior thought of reward and personal advantage. This instinctive certainty brings about supreme success and furthers through perseverance. However, not everything instinctive is nature in this higher sense of the word, but only that which is right and in accord with the will of heaven. Without this quality of rightness, an unreflecting, instinctive way of acting brings only misfortune.

It could be no more than nonsense of course but I was satisfied with my random throw. Oddly enough, the answer appeared to coincide with what was hidden. It was satisfying because it explained why Chey couldn't say no, why Pang merely did what she liked, and why Capon had a yen to garden in China. At once, this answer made me feel more relaxed about continuing. I was intrigued about encountering the unexpected.

Building people-to-people relationships

Conversation with Jocelyn Chey
9 JUNE 2017

Professor Jocelyn Chey AM was born and lived in Warwickshire, England until the age of 14, when she went on a long sea voyage. Seeing other continents provided her with a global perspective. In 1954, her family moved to Sydney when her father CJ (Kit) Milner took up the position of Chair of Applied Physics and head of the School of Physics at the University of Technology, Sydney (now the University of New South Wales). Jocelyn was the eldest of four children. Her maternal grandfather had been born into a missionary family in South India, and this sparked an early interest in Asia. Jocelyn was one of the first students of Chinese language and culture in Australia, combining this with history, classical studies and sociology.

Professor Chey has had more than one distinguished career. As a diplomat, she was the first Cultural Counsellor at the Australian Embassy in Beijing between 1975 and 1978. As an academic – a visiting professor at Sydney University – she lectures on Australia–Asia relations across Australia. Jocelyn is always on the front line of cultural developments between the two countries. She was the founding director of the Australia–China Council from 1979 to 1985. In 2016 she took up the role of Director of Western Sydney University's Australia–China Institute for Arts and Culture.

I first met Jocelyn in July 2014 when she opened an exhibition of a group of five female Chinese artists. Since then, we have kept in touch.

From July 2015, I had been collecting materials about encounters with Chinese art. When I approached Jocelyn in May 2016, she immediately supported the project and told me she would be happy to talk to me. We had many discussions. The actual interview was conducted on 9 June 2017 at Jocelyn's home. Jocelyn lives in a modernist Bauhaus dwelling overlooking the rocky landscape of Castlecrag on Sydney's Lower North Shore. The house blends in with the environment. As we talk, she often pauses and asks me to listen to the birds. 'Listen … I can hear one calling to another.' We started our dialogue with cultural relations.

ZU: In a recent public forum, 'Face to Face with China', you put the view that making connections with Chinese is actually about 'building people-to-people relationships'. This is such an important statement. There is a very similar Chinese expression, *renji guanxi*, meaning interpersonal relationships. Everyone associated with China understands the importance of such connections. They are a crucial way of getting along in China. However, sometimes people abuse them or bend their principles to do a favour for a friend. I am intrigued that you touched upon such a sensitive topic. Are you saying that the Australia–China relationship is built on relationships between individuals?

CHEY: To me it's very important to have people-to-people relationships. There's another expression, 'grassroots', that I don't like so much.

I really believe that in future, Australia and China will be very close. We will have a very good relationship, an important relationship. You can't just depend on the government and on trade because governments can change, trade can go up and down. There's something that comes, as I said, 'from the heart'. Otherwise, it's not going to last. It's just like a marriage: the parents can arrange the marriage, they can do that for political or trade reasons, but unless the two people love each other, the marriage won't be a success. That's my basic thinking.

ZU: Now I understand. The relationship you described is about establishing good relationships with respect and understanding. It is not *zouhoumen* [using backdoor connections]. [laughs]

CHEY: Let's go back to falling in love. First you have to get to know the other person. That means you must understand them. You need to know something about their background. You must know what they like and they don't like, and of course if one loves hot food and the other one hates hot food, then it will be very difficult to live together.

You have to find a way of getting along together.

ZU: I can definitely relate to that! Confucius says: 'A noble man aims at harmony and not at uniformity.' China's first Prime Minister Zhou Enlai (1898–1976) put forward a basic principle in building modern China's united front – using understanding and tolerance – seeking common ground while reserving differences.

Listening to what you just said, I think as a matter of fact, anyone can apply this ancient Chinese theory to all things.

CHEY: It's exactly the same!

To take my thinking a bit further, if we look at those art and cultural exchanges which have been successful, they have not been the ones which were arranged from the top. They are the ones, if I might say, that grew more organically from a community, or from an individual. Today I was thinking about the artist Huang Yongyu. He came to Australia in 1981, and I think he was really inspired by that visit. He felt a kind of freedom, which was still a bit lacking in China, perhaps. After he came, he wrote some poems, and he painted some pictures that were published in *Chinese Literature*. He was a friend of the editor, Yang Xianyi. You can see the actual results of that visit. I think it built into a new movement. It can't be said that he led the movement. He was already the older generation, but he was part of an important group of people.

ZU: How did you meet him?

Huang Yongyu (b. 1924) was one of the most influential Chinese artists of the 20th century. Huang was invited by the Australia–China Council in 1981 for the opening of 'Chinese Paintings of the Ming and Qing Dynasties'. To thank the Council, he gave them one of his famous ink and colour lotuses. The painting was on long-term loan to the Art Gallery of NSW. In 2017, with Jocelyn Chey's assistance, the Australia–China Council donated Huang's 'Lotus' to the gallery and now it's in the Asian collection of the Art Gallery of NSW. Jocelyn commented in her speech about this donation: 'Perhaps like the lotus, which stands tall and pure above the mud, [Huang Yongyu] felt that he had left the disasters of the Cultural Revolution behind him and his talent could blossom afresh. The visit [to Australia] had a profound effect on him.'

CHEY: The Foreign Languages Press employed a number of foreigners as translators. Huang Yongyu, Huang Miaozi,

Yu Feng and Ding Cong were all in the same group, a little circle of writers and artists. They used to meet at the home of [translator] Yang Xianyi and Gladys Yang [a British translator of Chinese literature]. We visited them regularly. Most times they would be there. The main thing was that we would bring whisky from the embassy. [laughs]

ZU: Your first interest in China, according to your autobiography, was aroused by missionary stories. But the real engagement with China took place when you were at university. You studied Chinese language and anthropology. What was it exactly that interested you about China?

CHEY: That it was different! [laughs] To be very frank, at that time I was a high school student sitting with my friend, and we were looking at the university handbook, deciding which subjects we were going to study. 'Oh! Look! There's Chinese!' (They were offering Chinese for the first time.) 'That'll be interesting. Maybe we'll just try it and see.'

In the first year, I took four subjects, so it was only one of the four. If it hadn't worked, if it had been too hard, or if I hadn't been interested, I could have dropped it. But at the end of the first year, I realised that this was another culture, something I was never taught about at school. Another world, almost. There was so much to learn and I was only just beginning! If I stopped then, I would have wasted my time. I still didn't know anything. So I had to go on and learn more! [laughs]

ZU: Studying Chinese language opened a new world to you.

CHEY: Yes. We didn't only study language. We studied the culture through the language. In fact, it may surprise you if

I told you that we started by studying classical Chinese. I was reading Mengzi (Mencius).

ZU: Really? The Confucian after Confucius? My goodness!

CHEY: [laughs] To understand classical Chinese philosophy, you have to understand about the history and the culture. It's not just knowing the characters.

ZU: Absolutely. You were more privileged than I was. When I grew up, teaching classical Chinese wasn't allowed at school. What exactly was taught in your day?

CHEY: I was taught in a very old-fashioned way. [laughs] I don't think there was much research into teaching methods. We read texts. In order to understand the text, we would ask the professor, then he would give some background, some history to explain the text. But it was all from the book.

ZU: Oh. That's sounds a bit boring. Were all twenty students able to do that?

CHEY: [smiles] The way they taught it was that if you hadn't studied any Chinese before, and you did one year of introductory, preparatory studies, then in second year, you could join the real first-year class. In that class were students who had studied Chinese before, who were mainly from Hong Kong and Malaysia. They had grown up studying Chinese and literature at school.

ZU: Ah. It sounds like you got into the Chinese group pretty quickly.

CHEY: There were four of us who studied together, and one of us, Jack Harris, started in the second-year group because he had already studied Chinese in the defence force. We continued all the way through to honours year and graduated together. We were very close.

Jocelyn explained that one of the remaining friends, Jack Harris, is now in his late 80s. He's written books about his experiences in the Army in Japan, Korea and Hong Kong, and in the intelligence services. Harris also published novels based on his life experience. He wrote his doctoral thesis at the University of Hong Kong and he made a special study of modern Chinese writer and poet Yu Dafu (1896–1945). He is also a good friend of Stephen FitzGerald, Australia's first Ambassador to China.

ZU: While you were working at the UK Regional Information Office, you met your future husband Hans [Moon Lin Chey] and married in 1964.

CHEY: Yes. He didn't have the name Hans when I met him.

ZU: Do you remember how your family and friends reacted to it?

CHEY: My family wasn't there. I was on my own.

ZU: You didn't even consult them?

CHEY: No. I didn't consult them. I just told them. I was a very bad daughter really. [said with a mischievous smile] If my children treated me the way I treated my parents I would be angry. [laughs]

ZU: Ha ha. Children often do exactly the opposite of their parents.

How about Hans? In the Chinese tradition, if a man wants to marry a girl, he has to ask his parents.

CHEY: His father wasn't there. He was in America. And he didn't get on with his father. So, like me, he didn't consult his father. [laughs happily]

> *I was amused by Jocelyn's story. While she was learning the culture, she literally renounced one of the basic Confucian moral principles – obedience. On the contrary, she was a feminist demonstrating the lifestyle of the new woman with confidence, being free to speak and act in the 1960s.*

ZU: So you two enjoyed total freedom.

CHEY: Yes!

ZU: How about friends?

CHEY: Our friends thought it was great! There were very few marriages between a Chinese and a European in Hong Kong at that time. And those that there were, were mostly a Chinese woman marrying a European man rather than the other way around. So we were certainly unusual. [smiles]

ZU: What a remarkable experience!

CHEY: It's interesting that one of the couples who got married in Hong Kong the same year as us was Pierre Ryckmans and his wife Han-fang [Chang]. Pierre died about two years ago.

Han-fang lives in Canberra and spends some time in Sydney. She and I feel we have a bond because we had the same kind of life experience.

> *Professor Pierre Ryckmans (1935–2014) was a writer, art historian and sinologist. He wrote extensively about Chinese art and was a great collector of Chinese art. In 2017, Han-fang donated Huang Binghong's painting 'Summer Mountain' (1940s) from their private collection to the Art Gallery of NSW.*

ZU: Did Hans have a lot of influence on your career or was your work separate from your family life?

CHEY: One of my conditions [smiles and corrects herself] – the only condition – when we decided to get married was that I wanted to continue working. I wasn't prepared to stay at home to be a housewife. And that was fine with him. In fact, at that time, because it was a colonial society, I earned much more money than he could. He was in business with his mother, so you can't really compare the two. My status in Hong Kong society was higher. It was … [pauses, searching for words] awkward, but funny if we went out together. If we went to a shop together, people would assume he was a tour guide and I was the tourist. They didn't look on us as a couple. [smiles]

ZU: Was he okay with that?

CHEY: We used to joke about it. We just took it as, you know, something ridiculous that oughtn't to be, and that some time in the future the situation would be resolved. He was a very open-minded … [laughs] you could say revolutionary character.

> *One of Jocelyn's later research topics was humour. Perhaps she found from her experiences that it is the most effective way to deal with pressure and complex situations.*

ZU: I wouldn't be sure I could handle that pressure. So, as far as career paths went, you remained independent.

CHEY: Yes. And all along I was the one who had a steady income because I worked at a university or in government. Hans was in business. Sometimes you make money and sometimes you don't. [laughs] It was quite a good arrangement, because often when both husband and wife are working, it's very hard to move from one city or one country to another. But he was more flexible. He was prepared to go along with me when I went to Beijing and find something to do when he got there.

ZU: That's really wonderful! No, actually, that's extraordinary!

CHEY: [smiles] I was lucky!

ZU: I think it was a stroke of luck for both of you both to find each other. It's not something that happens often, finding yourself in such happy circumstances. In most cases, people in this situation are put in a position where one sacrifices for the other. And because it is forced on them, it's an effort and the relationship doesn't last.

CHEY: No. We both benefited, learnt a lot, and gained a lot from each other.

In fact, we used to argue a lot. I used to make a joke when people asked why I got married. And I would say, 'Because I could never win the argument!' [laughs] So if we got married,

I would have more time to improve my Chinese, and maybe win the argument sometimes.

ZU: My goodness, the arguments were in Chinese?

CHEY: Yes! They had to be. When we met, his English wasn't good at all. Then he improved.

ZU: Do you see yourself as Chinese?

CHEY: Hmmm … There's a group of friends we had, including some people in Sydney who knew my husband before he knew me, who went school with him in Hong Kong. They say they regard me as being half-Chinese now.

I cannot see it myself. I haven't lived a normal life in China. When I was in China, my situation was privileged. So I cannot consider myself to be a Chinese.

ZU: Hmm, that makes sense.

> *I couldn't help but relate to Jocelyn's self-examination. It's a stance that fits with my interpretation: seek truth from facts. It is a truly scholarly attitude, which goes back to the Han Dynasty and remains valid today.*

When you were the cultural counsellor at the embassy in Beijing, there were several cultural exchange programs. Were you personally involved?

CHEY: Yes, I was. I want to talk about the first Australian art exhibition that went to China in 1976.

The exhibition was curated by Daniel Thomas. We had selected the paintings that we wanted to show in China. Each one was documented with a photograph, the name of the artist, the title and when it was painted. I delivered all the materials to my counterpart. There was no Ministry of Culture. It was abolished during the Cultural Revolution and hadn't been reconstituted. It was a cultural office in the Ministry of Foreign Affairs. They must have had their internal discussion, then they called me back and said, 'Each painting was considered separately.' At that point, they asked me some general questions and also some particular questions. For instance, the general question was, 'We need to know the class background of each artist.'

ZU: Oh, dear! Were you prepared for this question?

CHEY: No. That wasn't something that was considered at all in Australia!

They said, 'We need to know who it was painted for, and what was the intention.' They also said, 'We have some guidelines. There must be no violence.' So this painting of a highway robbery, a famous painting by Tom Roberts ('Bailed up' 1895), was ruled out because it was a picture of a violent confrontation. 'Also, no nudity.' Some of the early paintings – one was [John] Glover's 'A corroboree of natives in Mills Plains' (1832) show Aboriginal people dancing around a fire in a clearing in the bush – the figures probably had no clothes on … That one actually I managed to argue for, saying that they are so small, the painting is of the bush with very small figures, so you really can't tell. They did admit that 'if they are so small that you can't see the "details",' – they called it 'details' – [laughs] 'then we can accept it.'

Another painting was rejected because it was in a frame that had a branch of a eucalypt tree nailed onto it. So the frame was not a normal frame. They said it was 'too natural.' We let it go.

ZU: How bizarre!

CHEY: There were all kinds of strange rules. I really learnt a lot about China's art policy [laughs] – at least the Gang of Four, Jiang Qing's, art policy.

ZU: Hmmm ... times have changed for sure but unlike Australia, China still has art policies, as you know.

I learnt a lot from the Australian paintings when the exhibition came to Beijing, I was in high school, but I had already had received some formal training from family friends who taught at art schools. It was a very rare opportunity to see original oil paintings from the West in the 1970s. All we had learnt was from bad reproduction prints and Russian realist paintings. The Australians came before the Americans. I walked for nearly three hours after school to the Cultural Palace of Nationalities to see the show because I had to use my bus money to pay the museum entry fee. [laughs]

CHEY: It was really wonderful. I remember lots of art students went to the exhibition with their notebooks and stayed there the whole day sketching.

ZU: The Australian landscape exhibition must have planted a seed in me because later when I was deciding which country to go to, whether to choose America, Japan, Canada or Australia, I decided to come to Australia. The impression left by that exhibition made me feel I could relate to this place and develop my art.

CHEY: [laughs] So I played an important role in your life!

ZU: Indeed! Very important! Because art speaks more truthfully than words.

CHEY: The Whitlam government established the Australia Council to manage grants for cultural activities both in Australia and overseas. The director of the Australia Council, Jean Battersby, was a very important figure in managing these cultural exchanges. She had already visited China (1974) before I went to work in Beijing. They had agreed there would be a cultural exchange, and that was done by each side presenting a list of proposals. Then the other side selected what they would like. There was something in music, art and literature. Under the Australia Council there was a Visual Arts Board, and Daniel Thomas was a member. Daniel curated this exhibition. The Australia Council knew there were lots of political sensitivities in China because it was still the Gang of Four era. They thought landscape would be a safe approach because it would be more about nature than people. That's why they proposed it. It was the first time they had ever sent a comprehensive exhibition of Australian art overseas. A lot of thought and planning went into it.

Jean Battersby, AO (1928–2009) was an Australian arts executive and adviser, and the founding chief executive officer of the Australian Council for the Arts in 1968.

ZU: Were you the one who made the arrangements for the cultural exchange program?

CHEY: It wasn't me. It was Stephen FitzGerald who advised them.

The other successful outcome was from the Chinese Archaeological Relics exhibition in 1977. It was one of the biggest exhibitions to come to Australia at that time. It actually led to a decision to set up an exhibition corporation. Bob Edwards was the director of the Aboriginal Arts Board under the Australia Council. He put a huge amount of time into managing that exhibition. Insurance and freight were particularly difficult to organise. So they decided that this was more than the Australia Council could manage. We needed to have a separate body just to manage the exhibitions. That was an unexpected consequence of the Australia–China cultural exchange programs.

> *Dr Robert Edwards, AO FAHA (b. 1930), who grew up in Adelaide, was a curator, researcher, planner and museum director with a broad knowledge of anthropology, archaeology, Aboriginal heritage and art history. Bob made a remarkable contribution to the cultural sector in Australia. As a founder and administrator of Australia's largest exhibition touring agency, Art Exhibitions Australia (1990–2000), he developed new exhibition management practices and brought many significant exhibitions to Australia. The 'China's Entombed Warriors' (1982) was the first international exhibition managed by the agency.*

How about the Chinese Relics Exhibition in 1977? It attracted 600,000 visitors. That's a huge number for Australia. How did you work with the Chinese on that exhibition?

CHEY: The archaeological relics exhibition was different. Because China had already sent a similar exhibition overseas to France, Europe and America, our side was not prepared to accept an exhibition which was of a lower quality or less status than those which had gone to other countries.

ZU: Ha! Sounds like it was Australia's turn to call the shots.

CHEY: That was the main argument. For instance, they didn't want to send the famous jade suit.

ZU: I thought it did come.

CHEY: We argued about it! They were not prepared to let it out at first.

ZU: I'm glad you insisted! The Princess's Jade Burial Suit is the most important and one of the best China has. Now China has decreed that it is a first-class cultural relic, so the Princess is no longer allowed to leave China. [smiles]

I think it was the jade suit that brought Edmund Capon to Australia. Then, later on, he returned and stayed in Australia.

CHEY: Yes. He was asked to come to see it and write a catalogue for it. He wasn't involved in the negotiation. But he must have fallen in love with Australia.

ZU: It seems China created opportunities to bring people together.

CHEY: Isn't that wonderful! [laughs] I never thought of that! I must tell him that I played a very important role in his life!

ZU: Exactly! It's another successful example of people-to-people relationships. Sometimes it's direct, sometimes, it's indirect. It is also a very Chinese way to build relations.

Since 1950, the US and other Western countries had imposed a full-scale embargo on China. China's foreign trade had to be carried out under a closed and semi-closed economic model. However, in 1971, American journalist Edgar Snow and his wife were invited to inspect the National Day parade side by side with Chairman Mao in the tower of Tiananmen Square. The People's Daily published their photograph on the front page. This important photograph signalled to the Western world that China was not content with being left off the global stage. China established many diplomatic relations with Western countries in the 1970s.

Australian and Chinese diplomatic relations were established on 21 December 1972 under Gough Whitlam's government. Stephen FitzGerald (b. 1938) was the first Australian ambassador to China between 1973 and 1976. He played an extremely important and special role in Australia–China relations.

Let's talk about Stephen FitzGerald. You worked very closely with him in the 1970s on art and cultural exchanges. As I have been working on this book, studying each of you, I have come to realise that you are all in the same circle.

CHEY: He took on the role of first ambassador. He very quickly realised that they were going to need a member of staff to look after cultural exchanges. He should be given credit for persuading Canberra that such a staff position was needed in the embassy. At that time, the only place which had a cultural attaché was our embassy in Tokyo. It was not a common thing for an embassy to have someone in charge of culture.

> *Stephen FitzGerald has a broad expertise on international issues. He exhibits a unique personal analysis. To a less sensitive Westerner, messages from the Chinese government that were communicated via art were too awkward a medium. However, they imparted truth and political intention. FitzGerald identified the fact that cultural exchanges between China and Australia would enhance diplomatic and trade relations.*

ZU: I am sure there was good reason for having a cultural counsellor.

CHEY: At that time, I was working in the Department of Trade. Stephen knew me. He contacted me and asked if I'd be interested to apply for the position he created. It was unusual for someone to transfer from one department to another. So that was that.

Once I was in Beijing, I found that actually my job was much more than just culture. For instance, I was supposed to look after all the students and teachers, and also to cover science. It was very busy. There was a lot to do.

ZU: A broader sense of culture.

CHEY: Yes. The embassy had a very small staff. We were all very busy. I felt Stephen was very supportive and interested, but he was also quite happy to leave me to run it. [laughs]

ZU: He trusted you. That's where the person-to-person relationship counts.

CHEY: He was always there.

The most memorable thing we did together was not long before he left. In 1976, at the time of the smashing the Gang of Four, the Vice Minister of Culture Liu Qingtang was going to pay an official visit to Australia. We talked about the program. As was our usual practice, we arranged a dinner to meet the whole delegation. We decided to hold it at the famous Hongbinlou in Beijing. It was one of our favourite places.

We both laughed because Hongbinlou restaurant was a famous venue for Chinese Communist Party leaders, such as Liu Shaoqi, Zhou Enlai, and Li Xiannian when hosting banquets for foreign national leaders. Jocelyn was pointing out that this dinner meeting was very special.

It was arranged for 6.30pm because people liked to eat early in those years.

ZU: So you could and eat and drink the whole night.

CHEY: No, no no! The restaurant wanted you to leave before eight. The staff started to clear up then, putting the chairs on the tables. There was no sitting and drinking. It was all very formal.

We arrived and waited. The guests didn't come. It was seven o'clock and the hotel staff were getting anxious because they wanted to go home at eight.

We knew there was a lot going on. We'd heard that Yao Wenyuan, who was in Shanghai, had been arrested. There were funny things going on and we didn't know what was happening. I had arranged everything but Stephen came because it was his role as Ambassador to support it. He was anxious to get back to the office to see if there was more news about political developments. He asked, 'Shall we wait for these people?' It was very unusual for official guests not to come. Usually they were ten minutes early, not ten minutes late. But they didn't come. Sometime after seven o'clock, a young man who we'd never met before arrived. He was very hot and bothered and said he'd come on his bicycle from the Ministry of Culture. He said, 'They are not coming. I am coming down here to tell you that they've been arrested.' [laughs] 'Oh!' That was quite exciting news. 'The dinner is over then,' I said. But he said, 'No, no! There are other people are coming! They are just organising a car.'

ZU: Who were the other people?

CHEY: They were people from the Ministry of Culture. They came and they were so happy! They were happy because the Gang of Four had been smashed! They were determined that they were going to celebrate! [laughs] So we had the most relaxed and exciting dinner I've ever had in China!

ZU: Were you also very excited about the change?

CHEY: Yes! We didn't know what it meant. But it had to be good! [laughs] You couldn't be sure of the long-term implications.

ZU: So you just went along with it.

CHEY: Yes.

One of the guests said: 'For ten years I have not been allowed to read anything in English or to speak it. But I have been reciting Shakespeare to myself all this time. So, if you don't mind, I would like to recite a Shakespeare sonnet.' It was 'Shall I compare thee to a summer's day?' And the other man said, 'My favourite Western musician is Paul Robeson. Do you mind if I sing "Ol' Man River"?' So, one thing led to another, and more wine. Stephen threw himself into it, singing, reciting and drinking. He loved that kind of occasion.

ZU: You all responded spontaneously!

CHEY: Yes! It was the first time we had dinner that wasn't all about formalities. There were so many rules under the Gang of Four. People weren't allowed to talk about personal things. This was a real breakthrough. [laughs] The other thing that occurred to me later was how fortunate we were because if it had just been one or two days earlier, the Vice Minister and his delegation would have been in Australia at the time that the Gang of Four were arrested. That would have made for all kinds of political complications.

ZU: Did anyone eventually come?

CHEY: No. They just cancelled.

> *At the time of interview, I didn't understand what Jocelyn was trying to convey in her memories of Stephen FitzGerald. Afterwards I realised that she used this as small example of how FitzGerald personally handled relations with the People's Republic of China, especially the sudden change of circumstances. It resonates with what she stated in one of her speeches 'Forty years of cultural exchanges: how we got to where we are today'*

(2017): 'Nothing is worth doing, and nothing will be effective, unless it comes from the heart.'

We had a good laugh together. Jocelyn made some coffee for us and offered me some biscuits. When we resumed, we moved on to the time after Jocelyn returned to Australia from Beijing.

ZU: You were the founding Executive Director of the Australia–China Council from 1979 to 1985. At the end of your term, you said that at that point, the Council should have 'disappeared'. What happened?

CHEY: Well, I do believe with government bodies you need to have clear objectives. You need to say this is how we measure our work. Has it been successful or not? You shouldn't just assume because a government body has been set up that it needs to go on and on forever. That's why I said at the end of my five years there, 'I think we have achieved everything we set out to achieve.'

ZU: Obviously, the Australia–China Council continued.

CHEY: Because it was so successful, lots of other countries observed it and saw it was good. So they said in Canberra, you should have an Australia–India Council, an Australia–Indonesia Council, etc., etc.

ZU: You set up a model.

CHEY: Yes. It became a model for many other similar bodies. In order to rationalise that, later on, with budget cuts, the Department of Foreign Affairs put them all under one office. There was no separate secretariat for the Australia–

China Council. The one secretariat had to serve them all. So it doesn't have the same kind of unique status now that it had when it was set up. To begin with, we argued that this was necessary in the case of China. China is still a priority for Canberra, but ... things have changed. Not so much with what has happened in China, but with what has happened in our relations with whole of Asia, particularly in our region.

ZU: From the early days of the diplomatic relationship between Australia and China to the current state of art and culture, what has changed?

CHEY: What has changed in the past 40 years is there has been more movement of people between Australia and China. I think we didn't pay so much attention to the role of Chinese-Australian people in Australia as a kind of an intermediary. Individuals can play a very important role in developing people-to-people relationships. We have, for instance, Contemporary Asian Australian Performance and the 4A Centre for Contemporary Asian Art showcasing the works of Australian and Chinese and Australian Asian artists. This didn't exist 40 years ago. That's really been a big development.

ZU: They are also shifting the focus from China to a broader Asian perspective. Not that I think that's a problem, but it is sometimes confusing because when things are blended together, in my view, this integration comes with a loss of identity.

CHEY: It is a problem. For instance, my institute is called the Australia–China Institute for Arts and Culture, but it's Chinese culture, not just China. We still have to come to terms with the fact that China is so big that it is almost like Europe, it is so different from one area to another. And also, it's not just Han Chinese. There are included so many minorities, with their own cultural conditions. On the other hand, how do we include Taiwan, Hong Kong, Vietnam, Singapore and other places where there's Chinese culture? We must avoid making the definition too narrow or too broad.

We still have to come to terms with this. And of course it becomes a political problem too. For instance, if we are going to organise an exhibition with Taiwanese artists, they might not like to be called Chinese and might want to be identified as Taiwanese.

ZU: That's a problem that goes beyond art but it could open new possibilities if it's handled the right way.

For the past 45 years, you have worked constantly taking on many roles to solve problems as they arose, and you had people around you working towards to similar goals, to extend the understanding between two cultures. Do you think maintaining people-to-people relationship brings about continuity in cultural exchange?

CHEY: I keep in contact with a lot of people. In the early days, we were a small group. It was very new, we were younger, all very enthusiastic. We do keep in touch with each other but I wouldn't say I know everybody.

Jocelyn talked about the people she stays in touch with, such as Stephen FitzGerald, Ross Maddock, Nicholas Jose, Claire Roberts and others. Then I asked my last two questions.

ZU: China was very closed at the time you first went there. Now it is very open. You can come and go as you wish. Do you think China is as mysterious as ever? To me, it is.

CHEY: It's the same with any kind of knowledge. The more you know, the more you realise you don't know. It's commonly said about China that if someone goes there for a visit for two weeks, they will write a book; if they go there for two years, they might write an essay; and if you've been there for twenty years, you give up! [laughs]

ZU: Silence speaks loudly!

Earlier this year, you took up the position as founding Director of the Australia–China Institute for Arts and Culture. Why?

CHEY: Why? Because I am very bad at saying no. [laughs loudly]

Jocelyn talked about her busy life as a director at ACIAC and the many things she does outside Western Sydney University but closely related to Chinese art and culture, including medicine, sports, cultural issues, education programs, music and literature. Although she is so busy, she said she really enjoys doing it, because it is about building the foundation for a long-term relationship.

Our conversation has been filled with laughter. Appropriately, it concluded with laughter.

Resonating with traditional Chinese attitudes

Conversation with Mae Anna Pang
22 FEBRUARY 2017

Dr Mae Anna Pang was born in Guangdong, China and grew up in Canada, where she received her BA (honours) in Fine Arts and an MA in East Asian Studies from the University of Toronto. She received a one-year scholarship from the University of California and then a four-year scholarship from the Canada Council to study for a PhD in art history at the University of California, Berkeley. She studied Western art before specialising in Asian art.

Edmund Capon introduced us in November 2016. She and Edmund went to China in 1980 and held the first Chinese painting exhibition from China in Australia in 1981. At the time, Mae Anna Pang held the position of Curator of Asian Art at the National Gallery of Victoria, Melbourne. Since then, other well-known Chinese art exhibitions she has curated include: 'Dragon Emperor, treasures from the Forbidden City' (1988), 'Three Perfections: Poetry, Calligraphy and Painting in Chinese Art' (2013), and 'A Golden Age of China – Qianlong Emperor, 1736–1795' (2015).

I spoke with Mae Anna over the phone and we exchanged a few brief emails. She said she would be happy to talk to me about the Chinese painting exhibition. On 22 February 2017, I flew to Melbourne to meet her. She took me to a room that was about 9sqm, pulled a chair half-way out from a desk between stacked books and invited me to sit down. It was the office of Mae Anna, the Senior Asian art curator of National Gallery of Victoria.

During our conversation, Mae Anna spoke so extensively about art history that it isn't possible to include it all in this text.

ZU: Before we talk about the first Chinese painting exhibition in Australia, could you tell me briefly about your last show at the NGV, 'A Golden Age of China: Qianlong Emperor, 1736–1795'? It's the first major exhibition that the National Gallery of Victoria has held in collaboration with the Chinese government.

Mae Anna Pang curated 'A Golden Age of China: Qianlong Emperor, 1736–1995'. It exhibited from March to June 2015 at the NGV. The Minister for Creative Industries, Martin Foley, commented that 'The exhibition comes here as a result of the strong contemporary relationship between China and Victoria'.

PANG: Not quite. We arranged the exhibition of 'Dragon Emperor, Treasures from the Forbidden City' from the Palace Museum in Beijing at the National Gallery of Victoria in 1988 and it travelled to the Art Gallery of NSW in Sydney and the Art Gallery of Western Australia in Perth.

… the Qianlong show … I spent five years on it. It was a big project.

ZU: It was! What was also interesting was that through the exhibition, people could find out how Western culture was infused into Han Chinese culture.

PANG: I wanted to do just one emperor, the Qianlong who ruled from 1736–1795 during the Qing dynasty (1644–1911). And then I also wanted to involve Castiglione, the Italian [Jesuit and painter]. This has appeal for a Western audience and I liked the idea that the Manchu who conquered China in 1644 became Chinese and thus the conqueror became the conquered. [laughs]

ZU: I think the way you used multiple layers, for example, Qianlong's governing, social and historical context, built cultural awareness and helped Australians understand Chinese art in the mid-18th century under the influence of Western art. In a sense, the approach of reexamining the ways Chinese art has changed over time was very contemporary.

What also fascinated me was the natural flow from the Qianlong exhibition tracing back to the 1981 exhibition, 'Chinese Paintings of the Ming and Qing Dynasties'.

How did you get involved with the first Chinese painting exhibition in Australia?

PANG: I was just finishing my PhD thesis for Berkeley. I was doing it with Professor James Cahill.

ZU: The American art historian?

PANG: He was one of the best people at Berkeley – and Professor Wen Fong at Princeton University – on Chinese painting.

ZU: Cahill was pretty much the top authority in the world, as I heard.

PANG: I did my thesis on Wang Yuanqi (1642–1715) and Dong Qichang (1555–1636). So, it was just luck …

Jean Battersby asked me who I would recommend to do the exhibition and I said 'James Cahill'. They approached him, and he said 'Ask Mae Anna.' [laughs]

ZU: Ha ha! He sent the recommendation back to you!

PANG: Yes. So, out of the blue … Actually, it was better to do it then than now because I was in the middle of my study of the paintings of the Ming [1368–1644] and Qing dynasties [1644–1911].

ZU: Aha! That makes sense. So it was part of your territory.

PANG: Yes. James Cahill began by specialising in Ming and Qing. Professor Wen Fong was still focusing on the earlier periods of Song (960–1279) and Yuan (1279–1368). The Metropolitan Museum in New York was very interested in collecting Song and Yuan.

A lot of works came from CC Wang. He was from Shanghai and went to New York in 1949. He became a real estate agent, as well as an artist, collector and dealer. He would live in an apartment, then renovate it to sell. Most of the great Ming and Qing paintings in American museums came from him. And we, the National Gallery of Victoria, acquired paintings by artists such as Dong Qichang, Bada Shanren (1626–1705), Kuncan (1612–c.1674) and Wang Gai (c.1677–1705) from him.

So I was just at the right place, and I guess … the right time.

ZU: Right.

PANG: Edmund [Capon] was involved with the exhibition of Chinese paintings of the Ming and Qing dynasty in 1981. Have you heard of Bob Edwards?

ZU: He was another person from the ICCA [International Cultural Corporation of Australia].

PANG: It was Bob's first exhibition. This organisation now has Carol Henry working in it.

They were going to arrange it for five museums in Australia. It was the first painting exhibition from China. And it was the first time works from 35 museums [12 museums according to the exhibition catalogue] in China had been exhibited internationally – the first time in the world.

So I kept going. And that's how I got to know Edmund. We travelled together to China in 1980, with an Australian photographer.

ZU: The show was in 1981, so you put it together very quickly.

PANG: We went to Hong Kong. Then we took the train from Hong Kong, Shenzhen, to Guangzhou. It was so beautiful. There were gum trees, like Australia. I bought a lunch box of Hainan chicken. It was so delicious. [laughs]

ZU: It must have been since you remembered it so clearly. [laughs]

PANG: Then we flew from Guangzhou to Beijing. It landed at midnight. Ms Wang from the Palace Museum was there to meet us. There were three of us. Because it was October, the Peking Hotel was fully booked by the meeting of the communist party...

ZU: That would be one of the meetings of the Central Committee of the Communist party of China. They usually take place near National Day in October.

PANG: Anyway, she took us from hotel to hotel to find rooms. She hadn't booked for us.

ZU: Goodness me!

PANG: It was interesting. It was so dark. And the cars ... you know, if there were no cars coming from the opposite direction, the driver would shift to the opposite lane. You know they didn't go by any rules. There were very few cars, lots of bicycles. They dressed in Mao suits.

Finally, we went to this hotel. I was lucky and was given a big room with an en-suite. But poor Edmund and the photographer had to sleep in a bedroom with other Chinese men.

ZU: My goodness!

PANG: And they also had to take a shower in the public shower with other men. That's why I admire Edmund! I heard he used to take the lords and ladies from England to China. But this trip, he didn't seem to mind.

ZU: Right!

PANG: We said to the people at the counter, who were university students, 'When there's a room empty, would you let us know?' Anyway, they must have regarded me as an outsider. I'll tell you what happened.

ZU: What happened?

PANG: A couple of days later, I asked them again whether there was a room for Edmund. They said, 'Yes, there was one but you weren't here.' So they didn't reserve it for us.

ZU: Huh?

PANG: I thought, that's very hard to understand. Later on, there were rooms in the Peking Hotel.

ZU: Phew!

PANG: We met the curator Xu Zhonglin and the conservator, whose name I don't remember, from the Palace Museum. They had their own photographer. We were supposed to look at all the paintings.

ZU: They brought the original paintings for you to look at?

PANG: Yes, yes. Now, looking back … we were very, very … lucky!

ZU: Indeed!

PANG: Their very good photographer took all the photos. We wanted to take photos of some of them, but they told us that because they hadn't been published, we couldn't photograph them to publish them in our catalogue. On the other hand, they had already been photographed, so we didn't need to take photos again. It was really strange, full of contradictions, you know.

ZU: So, what they were really saying was, 'Do not take any photographs.'

PANG: That's why some of them were not illustrated in the catalogue.

ZU: I noticed that and wondered why! The text was comprehensive.

PANG: Edmund wrote on all the contemporary ones. I did the Ming and Qing.

It was really good working with Edmund because he let me do whatever I liked. When we were in Beijing, Edmund had already designed the cover. And Bob was very good. He made the decision about the hard cover.

The Chinese gave us all the Chinese inscriptions on each painting. They are quite difficult to decipher …

ZU: Very!

PANG: … the seal, poetry, cursive inscription. They told me they had 50 people reading the inscriptions in the cursive script of Chinese calligraphy and putting them into regular Chinese script for us.

ZU: Do you mean they translated them?

PANG: No. They didn't translate them into *baihua*, modern Chinese. They just wrote them in the regular script which is easier to read.

ZU: Oh, I see.

PANG: You have to study classical Chinese. It was still in *wenyanwen*. They only put it into regular script. It wasn't translated and there was no punctuation.

I came in to work and spent all Christmas working on it. They gave me the script to translate into English. Luckily, I studied classical Chinese at university and with my father at home. He was a civil engineer and he had classical training. So I did the translations and sent them back to Canada to my father. He corrected them and sent them back.

ZU: What support!

PANG: I also sent the script to my professor, James Cahill, to have a look.

Without Edmund and Bob Edwards, the exhibition wouldn't have happened. They were so professional. I found that if you work with the right people, everything is so easy.

Actually, the book is better than what I do now. It has a bibliography and title translations.

ZU: Impressive. Was the catalogue produced before the exhibition opening?

PANG: Yes. After we'd seen the paintings, I prepared the catalogue in a very short time – a couple of months.

ZU: The Art Gallery of NSW opened the exhibition first and the NGV had it last.

PANG: You must be right. It went to five museums and Bob later told me they sold 45,000 copies [of the catalogue]

... BHP, who was the sponsor, gave their shareholders a discount on the catalogue. The shareholders paid only $7 instead of $10.

ZU: That's a brilliant result! Did any of the Chinese staff come with the exhibition?

PANG: Yes. A curator, Mr Xu Zhonglin and a conservator of the Palace Museum and an interpreter came and stayed here for months. I looked after them. I found them a place to stay and introduced them to my friends. There was a very beautiful interpreter. Everyone wanted to invite her to their homes.

ZU: Ha ha.

PANG: I took them to our holiday house at Sandy Point to see the countryside and walk on the beautiful beach with the view of the mountain range of Wilsons Promontory. They said to me, 'You have one house already. Why do you have another house?'

ZU: Ha! Did they ask that? I am almost certain that, by now, they would have more than one apartment in China. China is in constant change and I think the art reflects that.

PANG: When the National Gallery of Victoria did the exhibition the Dragon Emperor from the Palace Museum in Beijing in 1988, two teams of curators and interpreters came out with the exhibition.

The first team was southerners. The first thing they did they bought a sack of rice and vegetables. The second team was from northern China. They bought mincemeat and flour from a milk bar and made dumplings. They saved a lot of money so they could buy gold. They bought lots of woollen jumpers or sweaters, one dollar each from the Salvation Army to bring home to give as presents to friends. What a contrast!

ZU: Ha ha! The differences are to be expected.

Apart from looking after the Chinese delegates, did you have to do a lot of work to get people to see this wonderful show and get them to like the paintings?

PANG: Yes, because Chinese paintings were not easy for people to understand. Edmund was very good. He organised a symposium of international scholars. He gave talks. He made a big difference. For example, Professor Michael Sullivan from Stanford University, Chinese artists Huang Yongyu, Wu Zuoren and his artist wife Xiao Shufang came, and the famous Chinese scholar and calligrapher Xu Bangda came from Beijing as well.

I gave a paper. My professor didn't come but Michael Sullivan told him it was good. Then I met all the important people: dealers, Dr and Mrs Frederick Baekland from New York, Mr Klaus Naumann from Japan, dealers who later helped me to acquire works of art for the National Gallery of Victoria.

Every time I went to the Art Gallery of NSW to talk about the exhibition of Ming and Qing, Edmund drove me to the airport. So nice! Can you imagine a director doing that! We also had Greg Burgess, the designer, who was a very talented architect. We had all the nice people working together.

ZU: Indeed! Why did you choose Ming and Qing for the first show? Not Song or Tang?

PANG: I don't know. *Mae Anna wrote me an email later, explaining what she thought the reason was:*

> Paintings of the Song (960–1279) and Tang (618–906) dynasties are mostly in the imperial collection in the Palace Museum in Taipei.
>
> Before the Chinese communists established Beijing as the capital in 1949, I heard that the American navy helped to ship the imperial collection to Taipei, Taiwan. Some curators at the Palace Museum in Beijing told me that sometimes the father or son, who both worked in the Palace Museum in Beijing, accompanied the collection to Taipei and they ended up not seeing each other again years later.
>
> As a result, there are very few Song and Tang paintings in the Palace Museum in Beijing and other museums in China. Even in the imperial collection in the Palace Museum in Taiwan, Song and Tang paintings are few. And from the Chinese point of view, they are ancient and precious, whereas there are more paintings of the Ming (1368–1644) and Qing (1644–1911) dynasties available and I wonder if some of them were collected by the museums in China from private collectors after 1949.

Later, on another occasion, I raised the same question with Edmund Capon. He said, 'We wanted Song and Tang dynasties paintings. But the Chinese said we couldn't have them. So we took what they could give to us.'

Anyway, the thing is, for the Chinese, painting is the most important, especially *wenrenhua*, scholars' amateur painting.

ZU: *Wenrenhua* – classical or literati painting?

PANG: Yes. But for most Westerners, they are difficult to understand and fathom.

ZU: That's probably because they haven't been introduced to the idea. They are unfamiliar to the eye and the mind. The West knows more about ancient objects like bronzes and porcelains.

PANG: Yes. They know them through auction catalogues. Actually, Chinese art is sold in a lot of auctions. They are very expensive now, you know.

ZU: Yes, I know.

PANG: But painting has a lot to do with traditional Chinese attitudes. The Chinese scholar and collector think that calligraphy and *wenrenhua* are the only form of art. Even the imperial art by court artists is not considered art. They are merely craft.

ZU: I can see their point and kind of agree. Chinese paintings reveal individuality and emotions while other forms don't.

It is interesting that the paintings were actually done by amateurs. The scholar-poets had their way expressing themselves. But I feel that Chinese paintings changed very little over time. Am I correct? They were very different to Western painters between the 15th and 20th centuries.

PANG: The paintings depend on the person, and their self-cultivation. Everything was more reserved. Even paintings by scholars like Dong Qichang look or appear very awkward. They seem bland and unassuming. But there's a difference between real awkwardness and apparent awkwardness. The scholar-amateur painting expresses the inner life of the artist with concealed brilliance.

Chinese personalities are like that – you do not show …

ZU: … you conceal the real self, somehow. I noticed you use the word 'awkward', do you mean *zhuo*?

PANG: Yes. *Zhuo*.

ZU: Like childlike.

PANG: Yes. That's right, you got it! They appreciate a childlike awkwardness and being natural. Even now, lots of Chinese – maybe not so much the young ones – are very bland and reserved. Usually the one who dresses well and runs around is not the boss. The boss is behind the scenes. Women don't wear makeup so you have to be able to see what's behind. In the same way, *wenrenhua* is simple – just ink and calligraphy or hand-writing.

ZU: Do you mean painting is not a personification, but a hiding place for the painter? I always find it rather difficult to read the blandness. It is almost tedious.

PANG: I asked the curator from Xi'an when we had the Entombed Warrior Exhibition in 1984 organised by Edmund, 'What's the ideal Chinese personality?' He said, 'Like a thermos, cool outside, warm inside.'

ZU: Absolutely incisive.

PANG: That helped me to understand the paintings.

ZU: Right!

Mae Anna then explained Dong Qichang's painting in detail.

PANG: Chinese do not show you everything. You have to be worthy of it. So, in a lot of Chinese museums they only show copies, not the real thing – except Shanghai Museum and Nanjing Museum.

ZU: I didn't realise that. I always thought the copies were all they had. Did the Shanghai Museum bring their real collection to Beijing for you to see?

PANG: Yes. They brought all of them to the Palace Museum. There were Nanjing paintings, Liaoning paintings … all brought in for the Ming and Qing exhibition.

You know [the paintings] aren't colourful, they don't have perspective, and they're not realistic. Human beings are not important.

ZU: Yes! That's exactly right.

PANG: It is so, so different.

ZU: What do you think was the level of Australian understanding or appreciation of Chinese painting at that time?

PANG: I didn't actually think about it. I just did what I liked. [laughs] I never tried to promote the work. I felt that I had to believe in it myself. I didn't have to worry because Edmund promoted it. All I did was to do my job, and what I liked. So that was really good!

The less I know …

ZU: … the more genuine you are!

PANG: Yes. You have to be! I think when people see the paintings, they have to resonate with them – in Chinese, *gongming*.

ZU: Do you mean for Chinese or Australian audiences?

PANG: Anyone! But you know, the beholder echoes with the artist. As the years go by, I see more and more in the paintings than I saw when I was young … as I grow and have more experience.

So, usually with Chinese collectors, if I visit them, they talk to me. For example, I went to Shanghai Museum in 1985. When they saw that I knew about art, they showed me more. Otherwise, they wouldn't have shown me.

ZU: How did you demonstrate that you were knowledgeable in this area? Did you ask questions?

PANG: I just told them what I saw. That's all. [laughs]

ZU: Make sense. Paintings are for viewers to see.

Did you request which paintings you'd like to see?

PANG: No. I was just given what [Shanghai Museum] wanted me to see. I trusted them and they showed me the best works. They also had a conservator and a curator. They hung the paintings. We were not allowed to touch them.

ZU: So you didn't have to do much.

PANG: No.

Back to the Ming and Qing painting exhibition. The Chinese museums selected excellent works, masterpieces. The paintings were from all different museums in China. When we went there, they had already done the selections themselves. They did a great job.

As I said earlier, Ming and Qing paintings are more available than the paintings of the Tang, Song and Yuan dynasties.

ZU: I know. But on the other hand, I think the exhibition provided an important introduction for Australian audiences to understand Chinese art. It was particularly significant in the sense that Chinese art was not static, but in a state of constant change. And to add to that broad knowledge, you provided in-depth analysis in the catalogue about artists like Wang Yuanqi, to allow audiences to better understand Chinese painting.

PANG: I was lucky because at Berkeley my professor concentrated on Ming and Qing, whereas at other universities, I might have focused on Song and Yuan and all that.

ZU: Your perception of the Ming, I find, is actually unique. When I prepared for this conversation, I read your essay.

[reading from the catalogue]

> It was ... no longer necessary for the Ming artist to go directly to nature to rediscover what the ancient masters had already discovered. Contemplation of nature was replaced by the contemplation of the art of the past.

You commented that 'style' was the central theme for Ming dynasty paintings. Did you mean the scholars merely studied from the masters' paintings instead of studying nature?

PANG: Yes, some of them did. For example, the Four Wangs, it was just style. Even now, they go by the style of the teacher. Maybe that's why some of the paintings aren't like Song paintings that are so close to nature.

ZU: There is a risk in studying secondary materials, isn't there?

PANG: Yes. That's why Dong Qichang had the theory of the Northern and Southern schools of painting.

For a few minutes Mae Anna continued talking about art history and comparing the schools after master Dong Qichang.

He says that you have to study paintings, then *hua* (paint), transforming it into your own work. One must not just copy.

ZU: Oh, I see. So you mean Chinese painting entails a gradual change from Dong Qichang's perceptions? I see in his painting more of his own feelings about nature. His paintings can almost be seen as nature instead of a representation of nature.

PANG: Dong Qichang used the Northern and Southern Schools of Zen Buddhism to compare the technical achievements [of the Northern School] in contrast to self-expression and creativity in painting [of the Southern School]. Shenxiu, a learned Buddhist monk from the north who advocated the Northern School in Zen Buddhism, said that you must study and work hard, like polishing a mirror, and not let the dust adhere. But Huineng, an illiterate monk from the south, said, 'From the beginning there has been no mirror. Where then does the dust fall?' In other words, the mirror is an illusion and therefore there is nothing to polish. In Buddhism, everything is an illusion.

Mae Anna talked more about Buddhism and Buddhist history.

ZU: In other words, the Northern school believed in gradual change while the Southern school believed a sudden awakening.

PANG: Yes. You are absolutely right! Technical achievement is gradual whereas creativity comes from within, like a sudden awakening. Dong Qichang employed this. It is not just a technical thing. To be creative you have to let it come from within.

Mae Anna went on to give a lengthy explanation of Buddhist theory. She expressed these arguments comprehensively in 'Mountains and Streams', an exhibition of Chinese landscape paintings she curated in 2006 at NGV.

ZU: Your role in translating all the text was very important. And the descriptions in the catalogue were very detailed. I quite like it that you expressed your own views in your writing.

PANG: Oh. That was just coming from a student, you know.

ZU: Well, aren't we all students? Like the old Chinese saying goes, 'live and learn'. The 1981 Chinese painting show was counted as a great success.

PANG: I was very happy with it.

ZU: I noticed an observation you made on the Ming masters, like Dong Qichang's landscapes. You commented that their innovation was 'highly expressive and individualistic'. And you went on to say, 'tensions are created by such disturbing elements as spatial ambiguity and juxtaposition, as well as by unstable forms.'

This is a very Chinese approach to aesthetics. How do you imagine Westerners would understand such complicated depictions?

PANG: Well, you would be surprised! When James Mollison was Director of the NGV in the early 1990s, I used to hang a Chinese painting in his office and say, when you are ready, please call me. I never told him what to look for but let him make his own comments. I once hung a landscape dated 1617 by Dong Qichang from the NGV collection in his office. He started looking at it and said he saw in the landscape forms pushing and pulling. So I was really surprised and impressed and said to him, 'Gee! You speak like Dong Qichang himself, except in English.' Westerners like the American James Cahill and the Swedish scholar Osvald Siren wrote great books on Chinese painting. I heard James Cahill at one time did research for Siren's monumental seven volumes on Chinese painting.

So, in a way, the Westerners, it seems to me, wrote better books on communicating Chinese painting. But the Chinese assumed their audience already understood it all.

ZU: That's true. We sometimes take our own culture for granted.

Did you acquire any Chinese painting after the 81 exhibition?

PANG: Yes, and also before. We had an American director, Eric Rowlinson from the Museum of Modern Art in New York. He was a registrar there. So he was very open to it. When Rowlinson was NGV Director, we acquired the Dong Qichang painting from CC Wang for $100,000. We used money made from the 1977 archaeology exhibition. Now it is worth $3 million.

ZU: I understand you regard Ming and Qing paintings as recent. I am also curious about the 21st century, contemporary brush-and-ink works. Chinese painting is merely a term to mark a distinction from oil painting. Before Western painting was introduced to China, there was only one type of painting – brush-and-ink painting. My concern is whether traditional painting will get lost.

PANG: Yes. It is possible. Now only a few people specialise in it.

ZU: Compared with the work you did curating the 1981 Chinese painting show, do you think it's more difficult now? Chinese art is not so unfamiliar to Australians, but from my observation, Westerners still find hard to harmonise and adjust their eyes and taste to Chinese art. In saying that,

I would not be surprised if not many Chinese people resonated with Chinese art either.

PANG: Yes. It's much harder. It is more demanding. You have to communicate with the public. The good thing is – it makes you try harder.

People don't have the time. [For the Qianlong exhibition] I gave more than 30 interviews to radio and television which reached a lot of people. The catalogue … [in a lower tone] they sold more than 4,000 copies of the Qianlong exhibition catalogue … But the Ming and Qing book sold 45,000 copies.

ZU: Are there other ways measure success?

PANG: They count attendances. I heard that the attendances at the Qianlong exhibition in 2015 was 67,000 visitors. But David Hockney's was 150,000 people, and the joint Andy Warhol and Ai Weiwei exhibition in 2016 had 400,000 people. You cannot match those numbers.

ZU: Hmmm … that's a challenge for Chinese people like us to contemplate – how to reinterpret, represent, renew traditional Chinese art. In my view, people do not appreciate the art as much as they might because they are not trying to have a conversation with it. In most of cases, people are looking without seeing, which it is really a shame.

If we forget about the numbers, the Qianlong exhibition provided an unprecedented opportunity for Australians to explore works from the Palace Museum's art collection. It was a very rich concentration of quality works, especially Qianlong's own paintings and calligraphy. I am glad you did it!

PANG: My secret is if you work with the right people, capable people, you don't have to do much. *Wuwei*, meaning 'no action' or 'non-interference' … you know … They just leave it to you, they don't interfere.

ZU: Yes.

How about the Dragon Emperor exhibition? It was also from the Palace Museum in Beijing.

PANG: 'Dragon Emperor: Treasures from the Forbidden City' was in 1988. I was on my own.

ZU: Right.

PANG: Look, this is the Dragon Emperor exhibition catalogue. The photographer of the Palace Museum, who did the photographs of the Chinese painting show, did this one too. Nancy Staub, who was Deputy Director of the NGV at the time, organised it. Patrick McCaughey was the director. He went to Harvard to lecture in Australian studies. Nancy Staub worked at the Metropolitan Museum in New York before she came to the NGV. She was wonderful and very supportive.

Every time the Palace Museum sent their curators here, they lived here. I looked after them, to establish a good relationship. I bought them chocolates. [laughs]

ZU: Ha ha. Chocolate sounds good.

At the end of our conversation, Mae Anna gave me some of her exhibition catalogues to keep. On 27 April 2017, she told me that she was leaving her job at NGV. On 28 April, Edmund Capon made a special trip to NGV between his meetings in Melbourne to farewell Mae Anna Pang on her last day at work. Since then, Mae Anna and I have continued our discussion about Chinese art.

'There is something going on over there …'

Conversation with Edmund Capon
16 JANUARY 2017

Edmund George Capon AM OBE was born in London in 1940. A specialist in Chinese art, he was the first art museum director in Australia with expertise in Asian art. Edmund was the director of the Art Gallery of NSW from 1978 to 2011. Under his directorship, the gallery broadened its Asian art collection and opened a new Asian wing in March 2003. As an influential Chinese art scholar, Edmund pioneered exhibiting Chinese art outside China. He introduced Chinese art and culture to the Western world, in particular to Australia, from a comparative, historical and social perspective. He came to understand the Chinese aesthetic and became an authority. This included knowing the artists personally. During his many trips to China, Edmund obtained first-hand knowledge and resources. He is an expert in Buddhist art, calligraphy, painting and many other genres, including jade, ceramic and cave art. Despite the apparent absence of individuality in Chinese culture, he recognised personal qualities and sensibilities which are often overlooked. Edmund continues to promote traditional Chinese art in contemporary Australian society and extend its influence.

I met Edmund in 1989 at the Art Gallery soon after I moved to Sydney in 1988. My memory of the occasion is, unfortunately, rather blurred but I remember clearly that he spoke with delegates from the Palace Museum (*Gugong*) in Mandarin. Over the years, I observed more of his engagement with Chinese art. In 2015, when I was painting Edmund for the national portrait prize, the Archibald, he revealed some fascinating stories. I said to him that someone must record them. I soon realised that I was the 'someone' who would record his stories and those of many others too.

I had many conversations with Edmund about his encounters with Chinese art. 'Terracotta Warriors and Horses' is the one I have included in this book. This dialogue was conducted on 16 January 2017 in the study room on Level One of the State Library of NSW. The glass-walled study room was very plain: a large desk, four chairs and a clock on the wall.

ZU: There's no doubt that the 'Qin Shi Huang: Terracotta Warriors and Horses' exhibition was one of the most important shows in the history of Australian art museums, not to mention the role it played furthering Australia–China relations. However, as I was going through the archives, I noticed that there is not much by way of recorded information. The Research Library of the Art Gallery of NSW houses four rolls of contact sheet in black-and-white Ilford film and one roll of colour transparency film of the installation. From newspaper and publicity clippings, I learnt that the exhibition opened on 22 February 1983. So, how did the Qin Shi Huang show start?

CAPON: If you're talking about the show itself, it happened in December 1982. We first opened it at the National Gallery of Victoria.

ZU: That makes sense. It was a touring exhibition, wasn't it? The exhibition catalogue listed the dates of the exhibition, starting with Melbourne. It came to Sydney at the AGNSW – you had it for a while, about three months. Then it went to Adelaide at the Art Gallery of South Australia for one month, and finally the Art Gallery of Western Australia, Perth, which ended in September 1983. Is that right?

CAPON: No, actually, there was another venue at the end – the National Gallery of Australia in Canberra in December 1983.

This was the first time the entombed warriors left China for an overseas exhibition.

ZU: As I understand it, there were only nine figures. But it was still the biggest show outside China.

CAPON: Yes – it was as we understood it the very first overseas exhibition devoted exclusively to the Qin Shi Huang buried army.

ZU: How did the idea come about?

CAPON: It happened after we'd done the 1981–82 Chinese paintings exhibition. The board of the International Cultural Corporation of Australia, including Jean Battersby, John Lockhart, Bob Edwards, Jim Leslie and myself, were very keen on maintaining a continuing exchange and exhibition program with China and that would include sending Australian exhibitions to China.

The government said that we should be doing something special to acknowledge the tenth anniversary of diplomatic relations between China and Australia. So that's when we came up with this idea.

ZU: The idea of showcasing the first Chinese emperor and his army would have been exciting, but also risky, I imagine. How long did it take from negotiations to realisation?

CAPON: In a sense it was not really negotiated as we went to our Chinese colleagues with the very specific idea of the Qin Shi Huang exhibition – and once the suggestion was accepted it all happened with remarkable speed!

ZU: Why do you think the Chinese responded to your request so quickly given they had never done it before? Was it because you had been there a few times?

CAPON: No. I knew China, but not that well. But we knew of the opportunity and we suggested it and it went through. The first Ambassador to China Stephen FitzGerald was very helpful in our discussions. The Chinese said, 'OK, we will do this.' Of course, as you know, it just goes down the line. There were no questions or matters to discuss. The decision was made.

ZU: Typical, centralised China – indeed, it was not all that different from the reign of the first emperor. An authority gives an order, and the rest follow through.

CAPON: Absolutely. It went to the State Administration of Cultural Heritage. They said it would be done.

ZU: The idea clearly came as a result of your first-hand experiences. I remember you telling me about how you went down to the digging site soon after excavation started in, I believe, in March 1974.

CAPON: True. I was there for the very first time in September and October 1974 just a few months after the very first discovery.

Edmund brought out a diary from 1974, to check dates, and a photograph.

In 1974, I did my first group tour to China in September. I took a group of twenty people under the auspices of a serious art journal in England called *Connoisseur*. They organised cultural tours to various parts of the world – to Greece, Italy, Mexico – and they were dying to go to China. Much to my amazement, the Chinese agreed to let *Connoisseur* have a tour.

ZU: And they asked you to lead the tour, didn't they? You were one of the few people to have visited China. Were you there in 1972? I heard that you convinced a lot of people to come on your 1974 tour.

CAPON: Yes. It was on that tour that we went to Xi'an. I wanted to take my group to Banpo Neolithic site. It was really well excavated in 1954. They said, 'OK. We will take you there but as it is in the vicinity of Lintong, we will also take you to the site of the Xi'an Incident.'

Edmund talks horizontally, in the sense that he does not just discuss art in a vacuum, but places it in its context, whether that be its social, political or cultural surroundings. To me, it seems like his love of geography influences his way of thinking – a simultaneous exploration of breadth and depth.

ZU: Was it where the Xi'an Incident took place?

CAPON: Yes, where they caught Chiang Kai-shek in his pyjamas.

ZU: Ha! But he didn't stay captured. He escaped. The communists were very proud of the Incident. I remember being taught at school that it was a turning point in modern Chinese history. They must have thought that it would be more exciting for you to see that as compared to pottery, stones and bones from over 6000 years ago.

CAPON: Indeed, our hosts really did think the site of the Xi'an Incident was more exciting that a crusty dusty old Neolithic village site – even though that provided a great opportunity for us to learn about the 'wisdom' of those early inhabitants.

It was from the Incident site that one could glimpse the burial mound of the First Emperor.

And I asked them, 'Is that it?' They said, 'Yes.' And, then [pausing, then speaking mysteriously] out of blue they said, 'Hmm, look, you appear to be interested in all this … archaeology and that … There is something going on over there … They found something … If you want, we can take you over there.'

Of course we said yes and so it was that we were taken to a scrubby pomegranate orchard where there were three or four holes in the ground with archaeologists just digging at the soil, out of which were poking the heads of the very first finds of the first emperor's buried army.

ZU: So up until then, you were not aware of the excavation of the Qin emperor's tomb?

CAPON: No, I knew nothing about either the tomb itself or the buried army. We drove towards the mound ... and there [pointing at a photograph] we saw this! We took these photographs! Can you believe it!

Edmund pointed to pages 31, 32 and 37 of the catalogue.

These photos were taken by a member of our group, a librarian called Howard Nelson. Look at the pictures ... amazing! We had no idea what it really was and certainly no idea of what was to come. All we saw at the time were literally a few tiny holes in the ground with these heads sticking out. Look at it! [laughs] It was absolutely ... I had no idea, really no idea at all.

ZU: Did they explain that these were the Qin Shi Huang terracotta warriors?

CAPON: No. That was absolutely out of the question. They had no idea what was there. Nobody had any idea. They just thought that there were a few figures there.

ZU: Of course, I mean who would have imagined what would be discovered?

CAPON: And on that first visit we actually met the farmer who was the first to reveal the First Emperor's hidden army – Yang Xinman. I met him again in 2010 whilst making a TV documentary there ... he proudly showed me the certificate he was given as 'the first man discovered the eighth wonder of the world' [points to a photograph of Yang Xinman on his iPad].

ZU: Ah! He was one of the six farmers who found the tomb accidentally while digging a well. Did you keep track of the excavation progress following your 1974 visit?

CAPON: Oh, yes! I kept an eye on what was happening.

ZU: Was that through direct contact, or through the news?

CAPON: Through the news, although I went back in 1976 and 78 with other groups to see it. By 1982, the scale of the site and the discovery had become apparent. So I thought, let's go and try to do a show with these spectacular figures.

Then, the Qin Shi Huang exhibition became a project of the International Cultural Corporation [of Australia]. I was totally involved, along with Bob Edwards, with every process of the exhibition. As Mobil Oil had been the sponsor of the first major Chinese exhibition [The Chinese Exhibition held in Melbourne and Sydney in early 1977]. This exhibition was incidentally the reason for my very first visit to Australia in January 1977. The company was enthusiastic about supporting the Qin Shi Huang show too.

ZU: So you started to plan a show in Australia. And you believed that the Chinese would cooperate with you and let you show them here?

CAPON: Yes. There was a lot of political manoeuvring. We used the opportunity of the tenth anniversary of Australia-China diplomatic relations to argue the case for having the exhibition – this was a very helpful and our Chinese colleagues readily accepted the idea.

ZU: It sounds like the perfect combination of national responsibility and personal enthusiasm.

CAPON: Well, they wanted something to celebrate this event. And so, we came up with this idea.

ZU: I remember reading the *Sydney Morning Herald* archives – they quoted Mr Hang, who came with the exhibition, as saying, 'This is the biggest exhibit of the figures to leave China. It is the most important archaeological find in China.'

Edmund clarified that there had been two or three figures included in more general exhibitions in America and Europe in the late 1970s, but this was the very first exhibition devoted exclusively to the Qin Shi Huang exhibition.

ZU: How did you curate them?

CAPON: First we decided that the absolute focus of the exhibition would be the figures themselves; and with them as the focus to tell something of the story of the First Emperor and his founding of the Chinese empire.

Having visited the site a few times I became intrigued by those faces – they were similar and yet slightly different. There seemed to be about a dozen or so types that appeared to be the basic models based on ethnicity and status. It then occurred to me that as each artisan-craftsman was working on the finishing touches to each face perhaps they just glanced at their nearby colleague craftsman and said 'yes that face will do' ... There is an amazing degree of reality and individuality to each and every one of those thousands of faces ... even though they are consistent in just about every way. Even today, thousands of years later, we can still feel that we are looking at a face that once really existed. And around them we created something like a theatre set ... to give a dramatic presentation.

There were only about ten or eleven types known at the time. There were not many restored figures and we needed to have one of each of the main types of figures, along with some other related objects, including for example, ceramic tiles and bronze weapons.

ZU: The show featured water pipes for drainage, is that right?

CAPON: Yes, but those things didn't come from the site. The pottery bricks came from Lintong and Xianyang's museums, the bronze tally was borrowed from the Chinese Historical Museum in Beijing as well as a few bits and pieces to make the show a little bigger than it was!

To be honest, we only had nine figures from the site. We had to create this huge expectation of the show out of nine figures. So, all we did was present it like a piece of theatre. The real interest, of course, was in the figures. And around them we created something like a theatre set ... to give a dramatic presentation.

ZU: That must have had a big impact on the audience – the shift from art museums showing European art to this new horizon – a new type of art, Chinese art. In my view, although a large part of the exhibition was about cultural diplomacy, your contribution to scholarship in producing such a high quality exhibition cannot be overstated. Was the theatrical setting intended to give audiences an experience?

CAPON: That's right. But the first challenge was to get them here. Their journey started with them being packed into big individual boxes and being driven, not flown, to Beijing.

ZU: My goodness! That'd take a week back then.

CAPON: From Beijing, the figures were transported by air to Hong Kong and then on to Australia, carried by the Australia Air Force Hercules; the Air Force was very supportive, and flew the consignment around Australia, and finally on to Japan.

ZU: The Australian Air Force!

CAPON: Yes. They flew from Beijing to Australia. They were packed in blue boxes when they arrived.

ZU: Were the figures all in one piece? There is very little documentation in the archives about this, which made me realise how easily history can get lost – even somewhat recent history.

CAPON: The handling of the figures was very tricky since there was really no previous experience … When they arrived in Australia (at the NGV) we devised some adjusted parachute harnesses and straps to lift them. It was also decided that we would commission a theatre designer to construct a 'set' to display the figures, thereby creating a bit of drama … in retrospect I have to say that I do not think this was quite the best idea!

ZU: Was the set a representation of the excavation site?

CAPON: It was more like a scene from a film – more drama than reality! By this time with all the publicity surrounding the discovery the public know more about that than they did about the circumstances of the First Emperor's burial; so we did attempt to tell the story hence the supplementary material such as weapons, tomb tiles etc.

I think probably the worst part of the display were the glazed brown tiles on which the actual figures were placed ... they were simply awful ... but I don't think the visitors were put off since they were only interested in the amazing figures and really didn't notice that there they were plonked on what looked like modern bathroom tiles. The figures were standing on brown ceramic tiles. They were like bathroom tiles which were absolutely ghastly. [laughs]

ZU: Do you remember the opening?

CAPON: I do remember well the first opening of the exhibition, in the National Gallery of Victoria. There was great excitement and expectation, a large audience and the then Prime Minister Malcolm Fraser was to officiate. Just as we were having to meet all the officials, the PM and of course a retinue of visiting Chinese officials we noticed that the 'theatrical' backboards did not seem to be too stable ... the thought of the whole scene collapsing on the figures was a bit too much so some of us crept quickly round the back of the displays to sort of hold up these screens whilst the opening ceremony was taking place! It was all a bit chaotic to say the least ... but at least we got through it all with great success.

ZU: Were you behind the stage holding those boards at the opening? Ha ha – what drama! The audience probably thought that it was intentional, to create the effect of a moving image.

I was amazed at how lightly Edmund remembered his triumph in this important event. It was a major achievement in his early career in Australia as an art museum director. It occurred to me that, perhaps in his mind, he was really just dealing with problems as they arose.

CAPON: [laughs] The whole thing was nearly a disaster.

Anyway, it all happened and people flocked to it! Then it went on tour. With the inclusion of Canberra (National Gallery of Australia), the tour was just about a full year from December 1982 to December 1983. Over one million people in Australia saw it when the population was only about 13 or 14 million.

ZU: The attendance at the AGNSW was record breaking, wasn't it? Was it also a successful business venture? One of the records stated that the exhibition earned the ICCA a net profit of $762,053. Perhaps it paralleled your success with blockbuster exhibitions like Caravaggio in 2003 and Picasso in 2011?

CAPON: It really was a ground-breaking exercise because since then, these figures have become China's greatest ambassadors around the world.

And there was huge publicity surrounding all of it. Because Mobil was a major sponsor, big banners with terracotta warriors were at all the petrol stations. If you bought $25 worth of petrol, you got a free ticket to see the show. There were queues for two or three hours in front of the gallery. The gallery was much smaller back then – it was less than half its current size. And the queue went out the front of the gallery and right down to Mrs Macquarie's Chair.

ZU: I hope it wasn't raining.

CAPON: No, it was sunny. People set up stalls selling ice cream under umbrellas. All sorts of things!

More demonstration that Edmund was not a director who only sat in his office. If that were the case, he wouldn't know what was going on the streets.

ZU: Ha ha! Were you responsible for raising any money?

CAPON: Raising the sponsorship for the exhibition was really not so difficult … which is unusual! The insurance was covered by the Commonwealth Government; and since the show was always going to be very popular and travelling around the whole country. We were in a good position. Mobil Oil had sponsored the first big Chinese exhibition (in 1977) and that company was pleased to support The Entombed Warriors exhibition – to give its now populist advertising title!

ZU: It also set a precedent for the Art Gallery because such an installation had never been done before.

CAPON: Yes. It was real theatre. It was much more than an art exhibition. It was a great cultural experience. It was the equivalent of Tutankhamun's tomb.

ZU: Did you give talks?

CAPON: Gosh, yes! Everywhere. The media coverage was enormous in every city. Every venue was a rebirth of the whole circus. It was a travelling circus. [pausing and contemplating] It really was!

There was one hiccup at the first venue in Melbourne when they were setting up the show. Don't forget that even for the people who worked in these institutions, handling this stuff was all new. That's when the 'manic accident of the sword', as the Chinese described it, happened. It was the only complete sword to come out of the site. It slipped and broke. It turns out it had broken before.

ZU: How did they mend the sword?

CAPON: They just stuck it back together. It was easy. [laughs]

ZU: Did you go to all of the venues?

CAPON: Yes, because I had to set them up. And the Chinese were expecting that. They were here all the time.

ZU: Oh dear! I forgot about that. Did they stay? Did they change?

CAPON: Yes, for the whole year. They changed.

ZU: Did you see them much during the show in Sydney? Where did they live?

CAPON: We usually rented a flat for them to stay in. We used to look after them quite a lot. They came to our house. We took them out, to the Blue Mountains, and drove them around.

ZU: By yourself?

CAPON: Yeah, quite often.

ZU: So it appears the show was not just an art show. It was the first diplomatic art exhibition in Australia.

CAPON: Absolutely. It was a big landmark show. Obviously, it started in a relatively modest form here. From here, in December 1983, it went to Japan.

ZU: So they didn't return to China?

CAPON: No. Actually they went straight to the Tokyo National Museum in Japan.

ZU: When I was reading the exhibition catalogue, I noticed that it contained more material than the exhibition itself.

CAPON: Yes, extensive research was done at the time. It has lots of diagrams. Look here. [pointing to the illustrations on page 51] This is Pit No. 2 – it notes that the kneeling bowman had gesso paint on him. [The catalogue] extended the knowledge of the time as we knew that they had been painted but had no examples of it.

ZU: Were you the only person involved in producing the catalogue? I've read the credits very closely, and it doesn't list any other authors.

CAPON: I think I wrote the whole thing, obviously with lots of help [turning to the Acknowledgements page]. Here are the people involved.

ZU: I like the content of the catalogue. It isn't a standard exhibition catalogue, is it? It covers a broad range of topics: history, anthropology, philosophy, art and archaeology. The details of the construction of the figures, using the excavation reports of the Chinese archaeologist from Cultural Relics Journal (*Wenwu*), are important components of the catalogue. It feels like a stand-alone publication.

Edmund went back to talking about the figures, recounting how many they had. He ignored my question. But after I asked him again, eventually he came back to it.

CAPON: It was used as the catalogue for a number of years. I believe it was my text, from subsequent catalogues that I happened to see by chance, formed the basis for a number of similar exhibition publications in America, France, Scotland, Switzerland and Finland.

Swiftly, he resumed talking about the show.

To be honest, the hook we hung this exhibition on was to celebrate the tenth anniversary of diplomatic relations. Once this sort of politics gets involved, you can pull off things you couldn't otherwise do.

ZU: And of course, the legacy of the exhibition goes beyond just celebrating diplomatic relations. I can't wait to hear about your second Qin Shi Huang show.

CAPON: The second show was exclusively organised with Xi'an so there were big differences. First, we didn't deal with Wenwu Ju (the Bureau of Cultural Relics), we dealt with the provincial museums. The [1982] show was totally a political gesture – without the event of the tenth anniversary of diplomatic relations, it wouldn't have happened. You needed a political element to persuade the Australian and Chinese governments to take on something like this.

ZU: So political intentions were necessary to spread Chinese art and culture.

CAPON: Yes.

ZU: Do you think that element is still necessary?

CAPON: No. We can do without them …

ZU: … because understanding has already been fostered?

CAPON: Yes.

Our conversation ended here. One month later, I made another appointment with Edmund Capon to talk about the second Qin Shi Huang exhibition which showed at the Art Gallery of NSW in 2010.

'Let's do it again!'

Conversation with Edmund Capon
6 February 2017

ZU: The last conversation we had, you talked about the first Qin Shi Huang exhibition in 1982–83. It was exciting in the sense that it had never been done before.

CAPON: Yes, it was what we called it – a ground-breaking exhibition.

ZU: That's right!

CAPON: It was very exciting because we knew that we were telling a great story and we were actually the first people to tell this great story outside China and in a popular way.

ZU: Exactly! But, in 2010, 'The First Emperor' exhibited at the Art Gallery of NSW. What was the excitement for you this time? Hadn't you seen it all and done it all before?

CAPON: Yes, we'd seen it all, but … what was exciting about it? Well, there were two or three things.

First, when we did the first show, the full extent of the revelation of Qin Shi Huang's buried army was still in progress and, in a sense, it is still in progress.

By 2010, a lot, lot more had been revealed and it was possible to tell much more of the story. The public who flocked to the first exhibition had something of an appetite for the second show. And also, so many people who knew about the story, about this amazing find, of course were too young to flock to the first show.

I can remember talking to some young visitors in the gallery in about 2008. It was about the time we did 'The Lost

Buddhas' show. They were talking about China and Chinese art. They said, 'Why don't you bring that exhibition – the entombed warriors? We heard they had been around the world, to America, Europe and everywhere else. Why don't you do that?'

I said, 'Oh, I've done that!' I'll never forget that conversation.

[One of them] said: 'When?'

'In 1983,' I said.

Then she said, 'Edmund, I was two then.'

So I thought it was time to do it again.

> *To many, this brief conversation would have been easily overlooked. However, as a Chinese artist, I appreciated that such a seemingly insignificant question was responded to in such a grand way, leading to the 2010 'The First Emperor: China's Entombed Warriors' exhibition. It was a very 'Edmund' thing to do, in the sense that he relates big events to personal experiences. In my view, it resonates with the Taoist concept of spontaneity.*

ZU: So you helped the emperor live again. [laughs] That's immortality.

CAPON: Exactly! I agree!

It was at that moment, with those two or three girls in the gallery, that I said to myself, 'Let's do it again!'

As I made that decision, I thought we could do a much bigger show of the whole era, the history of Qin Shi Huang and the Qin dynasty. Although it was very much about the entombed warriors, it was actually an exhibition about the first emperor. So we called it 'The First Emperor'! It was about life at the time, art, and the culture of Qin Shi Huang and the Qin dynasty.

I feel the first show we did really opened the door. Since then, the entombed warriors, I think, have become China's greatest ambassadors.

ZU: That is all very true. What were the challenges in creating the 2010 show? After all, you knew the materials very well by then.

CAPON: It was always a challenge because … well, think about the different circumstances between the 1983 exhibition and the 2010 exhibition. All the new materials, for example – the horses and chariots had not been found at the time of the first show; none of the acrobats; the stone armour; and the beautiful bronze birds. So much had been found in … 25 years. It was 25 years!

ZU: Was there a different perspective that you tried to showcase at the Art Gallery this time?

CAPON: There was a different perspective because we decided that it would be a show about the personality, the character and the achievements of the first emperor.

The first show in 1983 was about this remarkable discovery.

It was just a glimpse – a tantalising short glimpse into this extraordinary discovery.

The 2010 show was much more. If you look at the catalogue, there's much more – a whole play, if you like, about the life and times of the first emperor, and his achievements.

ZU: Did you exhibit your show differently from the way China exhibited theirs? Was there a different emphasis or different focus?

CAPON: Obviously, all we could do was to try and evoke the site through the figures, and through the display of a wide range of Qin material, to demonstrate the story and the achievements of the Qin Dynasty. So, in this respect, the exhibition was an extension of the story of the actual burial site.

ZU: Do you mean you extended it to encompass his personality?

CAPON: Yes. When you look at the content of the exhibition in 2010, you'll see that we borrowed from probably eight museums around Xi'an. So, it was really to tell the story of the achievements of the Qin Dynasty.

ZU: What was the significance of showing this – the life of an emperor from 2000 years ago?

CAPON: For the very simple reason that his dynasty, however tyrannical it was, laid the foundations for the entire history of China over the last two millennia to the present day.

ZU: That's very true!

CAPON: That's why I gave these lectures, comparing … no, not comparing, but drawing parallels between Qin Shi Huang and Mao Zedong.

ZU: I noticed that Mao's images were used in the documentary you did for the exhibition. To be honest, I was puzzled about that.

CAPON: Why should you be puzzled about it?

ZU: Because it was not very clear to me … What was your standpoint?

CAPON: The standpoint was very simple. Qin Shi Huang was ruthless. He managed to defeat the opposition and actually unite the disunited empire. That's what he achieved. And he achieved that after centuries of warring states and periods of disunion.

ZU: True. How does Mao fit into this?

CAPON: Mao Zedong inherited a fragmented empire that had been raped and pillaged by the West for three centuries, and it was in disorder and on the verge of collapse. Only somebody as ruthless as the first emperor … only Mao could grasp that ruthlessness, actually destroy the opposition and create a new regime.

And the other thing is … Qin Shi Huang was such a powerful figure! He was a leader … for a very short time … and he created an empire. He led China out of centuries of conflict and established unity. But he was an instrument of change, not a leader for more tranquil times. So it was that the Qin Dynasty was so brief, just 15 years.

I think the ruthlessness created a stage, a platform for relative stability. After all, if you look at the achievement of Qin Shi Huang, his reign was followed by four centuries of relative peace, stability and growth in the Han dynasty.

ZU: Hmmm ... I see your point.

CAPON: My contention is that Mao, by completely redefining the Chinese stage, if you like, like his predecessor Qin Shi Huang, created a platform, a stage for a long period of stability, calm, and prosperity.

Could you have imagined what has happened to China in the last three decades? The entire world is staggered by China's progress in the past three decades.

Now ... I ask you the question, had Mao not been around to establish the People's Republic of China in 1949, what would have happened to China?

ZU: I don't know ...

CAPON: My perspective looks at what Mao achieved and then reflects on – or sees it as an echo of a kind of – what Qin Shi Huang achieved.

I just thought ... there's something in it! For all of Mao's eccentricities and excursions into extremism, he was very much a profound inheritor of the Chinese psyche and Chinese values.

It's about centralising power. Invoking the name of the first emperor somehow validates some of the things he did, such as his anti-Confucius stance.

One other thing that has always intrigued me is the timing. Because in 1974, wasn't there an anti-Lin Biao and anti-Confucius campaign – an echo of the First Emperor's anti-Confucius policy? And suddenly, we discover this amazing achievement of the first emperor? You have to say, 'Hello? Is this a coincidence or is this a kind of plan?'

> *I was intrigued by Capon's comments. When I returned to my studio, I took out the exhibition catalogue. It was an English–Chinese bilingual publication. I looked up his essay, 'The First Emperor: inheritance and legacy'. He addressed his view, drawing parallels between the Qin Emperor and Chairman Mao. Having missed this previously in my research, I realised that I must have only read the Chinese text – the Chinese version was a selective translation, omitting his comments on Mao.*

ZU: One question, if I could draw us away from the political – as an artist, I find that the restoration of the figures recent years has been somewhat overdone. I think they make them too perfect. The liveliness has gone ...

CAPON: This is the interesting thing! Because I have been there many times now – into the workshops. I have seen these piles and piles of broken ceramic figures. The idea that there is a complete figure is actually nonsense. It is almost impossible. And even the ones that are now composed entirely of genuine parts probably are often a mixture of figures – they have to be.

I remember the director, Wu Yongqi – this was when I was there in 2010 – saying that working at the Qin Shi Huang site where they do the conservation restoring the figures was not just a job, it was a lifetime career.

ZU: Right, a lifetime.

CAPON: It was a lifetime's work. Yes.

ZU: I remember you saying that when you talked to the director, he said that he was hoping the technology would develop so that they didn't have to disturb the deep long sleep of the emperor – to see everything without opening his tomb.

CAPON: Ah! On the tomb itself, for centuries, everyone knew that it was the tomb of the emperor.

ZU: Correct.

CAPON: The idea was well described in Sima Qian. Everybody knew what was in there. We had a fair idea about what …

ZU: Do you mean the mercury river, the candles that never go out … is that fiction?

CAPON: No, no! I think it is possibly absolutely true!

ZU: Right. How exciting would that be if we could see it!

CAPON: I don't know how true this is, but my feeling is [in a mysterious voice] Qin Shi Huang's tomb has possibly long since been emptied.

ZU: So they didn't want to discover this ... disappointment.

CAPON: They didn't want to discover a huge anti-climax. They open it and – guess what – the cupboard is bare.

But, on the authenticity of Sima Qian's description, they claim, and I have seen the documentation of this, that they tested various parts of the soil, on all parts of the mound, and they found unusually high levels of mercury in the soil. So that is possibly absolutely true, but still we do not know what treasure may or may not lie within the burial ...

ZU: It's the so-called silver river.

CAPON: That's the mercury. I am quite sure. The tomb was excessively furnished.

But, of course, what Sima Qian did not mention was first, the buried army, and secondly, the virtual city around the burial. So that's why those discoveries have been such a revelation. Obviously, the site where the two chariots were found was extraordinary. Then there were the acrobats and the entertainers. Then there was the pit of armour and the shale stone segments of suits of armour. Even further away, and this is the most recent of the major discoveries, is the little Arcadian river with the birds, and fishermen. So that whole city, the virtual city, has barely been touched.

Edmund was late for his next meeting. I quickly asked my last question.

ZU: There is one question I've always wanted to ask you. When you returned to the spot in 2010 where you stood 36 years ago, among the pomegranate trees, and saw the few holes in the ground, how did you feel?

CAPON: Oh ... hmm ... I felt like doing gardening in China! Because you will probably discover something! I think if I went to China, I would have grown vegetables and while digging them up, I would have found some ancient bronzes.

ZU: Ha ha!

Having been the director of the Art Gallery of NSW over 33 years, Edmund Capon's legacy on art has gone far beyond his encounter with Chinese art. This piece of memory would have been merely a small part of his achievement. And yet.

Chapter II

Before sorrow, anger,
longing, or fear have arisen.
you are in the centre.

Once you find the centre
and achieve harmony,
heaven and earth take their proper places
and all things are fully nourished.

Zhongyong (The Doctrine of the Mean) Chapter 1

Hold on to the Centre

Borrowing 'Hold on to the Centre', the Taoist principle for life, as this chapter's title signifies an act of infinite kindness.

This chapter contains five conversations I had with artists Guan Wei, Liu Xiaoxian and Ah Xian, cultural attaché Nicholas Jose and gallery director Gene Sherman. The narrative is built on the period from the late 1980s to the 2000s that started with China's opening up to the world. In its wake, enthusiastic young Australians travelled to China, the June Fourth Tiananmen Square Massacre took place in 1989 and following this event, Chinese artists arrived in Australia seeking opportunities to create freely. It is a case study of Chinese contemporary art sharing achievements and engaging with Australian society.

I discerned a connection between them when I was choosing the conversations to form this chapter. The dialogues I had with artists were about how their works were made, why they made them, and their meaning. Jose's stories of making friends with underground artists resulted in their introduction to Australia's mainstream art world. Sherman provides an account of being one of the first galleries to show contemporary Chinese art and to give Australian viewers fresh insight into contemporary Chinese society. They were seemingly doing different unrelated things. However, it became clear to me that the relationships they developed in times of hardship carried with them a positive energy for Australian society. Like those pioneers in chapter one, once they had established the new platform, the whole community was able to see China from a variety of dimensions.

To look more deeply into the legacy of these stories, I consulted the *I Ching*, asking 'What do these individual stories mean today?' I arrived at hexagram 28, *Da Guo*, or Preponderance of the Great. Wilhelm translates it as:

```
═══  ABOVE: THE JOYOUS, LAKE
═══  BELOW: THE GENTLE, WIND, WOOD
```

The hexagram represents a beam that is thick and heavy in the middle but too weak at the ends. This is a condition that cannot last; it must be changed, it must pass, or misfortune will result.

THE JUDGMENT
Preponderance of the great.
The ridgepole sags to the breaking point.
It furthers one to have somewhere to go.
Success.

The hexagram indicates that society is facing a time of collapse because the ridgepole, which the whole roof rests on, is tilted and too weak to bear the great weight in the middle. It is an exceptional time and situation, therefore extraordinary measures are demanded. It is necessary to find a way to transition as quickly as possible, and to take action. This promises success.

What I obtained from the 'Preponderance of the Great' hexagram is a life truth. When you see such a hexagram, you must follow two principles of the way: 'independence and fearlessness' and 'retreat and contentment'. You should insist on pushing ahead. Through friendly relations with people of lower rank, a responsible man can succeed in becoming the master of the situation but such conditions are temporary. When you realise you are unable to make progress and you are powerless to save a desperate situation, there is no shame in retreat. Alone, without complaint, you should devote yourself to self-cultivation.

As we see from the stories of Guan, Liu and Ah Xian, these artists completed their transitions quickly in Australia. With help from people like Jose and Sherman, they responded to the direction of the Tao. This could be a mere coincidence but in connecting these individual experiences – the this and the that, not opposing each other – we may find the centre, and in the centre of the circle is serenity.

'I was really lucky in Australia'

Conversation with Guan Wei
4 August 2016

Guan Wei was born in Beijing into a Manchu family in 1957. He studied fine arts at Beijing Capital University (1982–86). After graduation, he taught art at a high school. Guan Wei first visited Australia in 1989 and returned to Sydney in 1990.

Guan Wei is one of Australia's leading contemporary artists. He is best known for his distinctive style of painting that combines Australian and Chinese influences. He references symbolic images in his art to reflect Chinese and Western philosophies. Guan uses humour and satire to comment on contemporary issues through paintings, sculptures and installations. His seemingly light-hearted approach to socially divisive content inspires and opens viewers' minds to reconsider contemporary social issues.

Our work was shown together in several curated exhibitions but we only met in person in 2016 when we both appeared in 'Foreshadow' at Vermilion Art in Walsh Bay, Sydney. There, I had the opportunity to get a real sense of him.

On 4 August, Guan Wei and I had our conversation at the gallery while we were installing our works. I was particularly interested to talk with him about the turning points in his art development in Australia.

ZU: I'd like to ask about your transition period … How did you start to develop your art practice in Australia?

GUAN: Things started back in 1987 and 88 in Beijing when I met some foreigners, including Nicholas Jose. Nick was the cultural counsellor of the Australian Embassy in Beijing. He liked contemporary art, so he had artist friends. Whenever there was a delegation from Australia, he would bring them to us to see our work.

ZU: Can you share your memories of those visits?

GUAN: In 1988, the director of the MCA (Museum of Contemporary Art), Bernice Murphy, visited China. Nick brought her to my home to see my works. She was really impressed with their quality. They left a deep impression on her.

> *Bernice Murphy was Curator of Contemporary Art at the Art Gallery of NSW, Sydney (1979–83); then Curator, Chief Curator, and finally Director, MCA, Sydney (1984–2008).*

ZU: Did you show your paintings publicly during that time?

GUAN: In 88, Nick held an exhibition at his home for me, Ah Xian, Xiao Xian and Lin Chunyan. It was a like a salon, you know, showing paintings at a Westerner's home. There were many salons in Beijing in those days.

Around the same time, in October, an Australian art education delegation group came. Nick took them around China to visit art institutions. But the artworks were all merely copying realist and romantic styles because China wasn't that open at the time.

ZU: They were not excited by art that was so familiar to them.

GUAN: No. They didn't find it interesting. At that time, China was just opening up, and individuality wasn't yet encouraged. The artists with individual character were all underground. Because of that, Nick invited them to his home to see our works. He also invited us to come and meet them.

ZU: That's exciting.

GUAN: It was great! We went along. They were so surprised to see such work. They had never seen anything like it before. It was totally different from what they had seen in the art institutions.

I remember Geoff Parr, the director of the Tasmanian School of Art discussed post-modernism with us. He claimed that China had not reached that stage yet. Somehow, I started to argue with him.

> *Geoff Parr AM (1933–2017) was a photographer and art educator. He was emeritus professor of art and an honorary research associate at the University of Tasmania's School of Art and a member of the Australia Council's Visual Arts Board in 1976–78. In 1978, he was appointed head of the Tasmanian School of Art.*

ZU: Did you argue that your work was post-modernist?

GUAN: Ha ha! Something like that. Our English wasn't good. Nick and his assistant translated for us. We talked enthusiastically for over an hour. The atmosphere was great. Then the party finished, and we left.

One month later, we received a letter out of the blue. It was an invitation from the Tasmanian School of Art to me, Ah Xian and Lin Chunyan to take up an artist-in-residency.

ZU: Aha! Things had been planned for you.

GUAN: Ah ... that's right ... ha ha ... I had never been abroad ... What a wonderful opportunity!

We immediately started getting ready to go. The passport and visa application procedures were complex because we had to get approval from the Ministry of Culture and the Ministry of Foreign Affairs. Eventually it went through.

In January 1989 we came to Hobart for a two-month summer school.

ZU: What was included and where did you stay?

GUAN: It included return airfare, accommodation and a stipend. They also gave us funds for materials to make artworks. We lived in university flats.

It was so great. I made over 30 pieces of works.

ZU: Sounds like you were on fire with lots of artistic stimulation.

GUAN: Yes. Ah Xian made about 20 works. Lin Chunyan painted 40 paintings. He worked fast. We had an exhibition.

ZU: At the Tasmanian School of Art?

GUAN: That's right. Before we left, the director spoke to us. He had to evaluate our works. Geoff said I was the first Chinese surrealist artist. I was shocked.

ZU: He was clearly falling for your work.

GUAN: Yes, to my great appreciation. I was overwhelmed.

ZU: Ha ha! That was your 'Acupuncture' series, wasn't it? Geoff Parr was surely pierced! Your art has continued to build on that. How wonderful.

GUAN: [laughs] It was very obviously my style.

After finishing two months' residency, we visited Melbourne for three days. Nick organised everything for us. We had a host taking us around to see museums and meet people. Then we came to Sydney and we were introduced to Ray Hughes. We visited the MCA director Bernice Murphy because we had met her in Beijing. MCA was only an office at Sydney University then. We saw their collections.

ZU: Yes. It was the Power Institute.

> *The MCA was founded in 1989 to deliver the 'museum' aspect of John Power's desire to bring international contemporary art to Australia. The Power Bequest initially provided the core funding for the new MCA. Bernice Murphy wrote extensively about the bequest, the University of Sydney and the establishment of the MCA and its early years in Vision & Context, Museum of Contemporary Art, Sydney 1993.*

What brought you back to Australia the second time?

GUAN: Soon after I returned to Beijing in March, the students' democracy protests began. Beijing was in a chaotic state. Right after *liusi* (June Fourth), I received a letter from Geoff Parr inviting me back.

ZU: So he made the first move?

GUAN: Yes. He thought I was in danger and wanted to rescue me [laughs]. The media had broadcast that China was in terrible trouble, on the brink of a civil war. I wrote back explaining that the situation wasn't as bad as it seemed in the news. You know I had just come back from Australia and although it looked like chaos from the outside, people's lives were still in order. So I thanked him but didn't accept his invitation.

However, after a year, I realised I couldn't stay in Beijing. Everything was frozen, martial law was introduced. There was no cultural exchange, I couldn't go to embassies. That was the real kill. All the intellectuals in Beijing had escaped abroad.

So I organised a salon. I said, 'Let's not be depressed.' I suggested we meet at our homes. We would come up with a topic, then everyone would make a painting about it. Later, we would gather again to judge a winner. It was just a game to cheer us up. We had a few rounds and it went really well. Eventually, the foreigners came back, one after another.

ZU: Was this still 1989?

GUAN: No. It was 1990. Martial law was still in place.

ZU: In such an intense environment, your artistic inspiration must have been very high.

GUAN: I made a few series of works including 'Two-finger exercise' (1989–90). That's now in the MCA's collection. It was reflecting on June Fourth.

> 'Two-finger exercise' (1989–90) comprises 48 paintings, a number of short poetic texts, a series of collages of black-and-white photographs and Chinese envelopes. Guan describes the collages as 'certificates' that indicate 'a secret letter has arrived and there are hidden meanings to be opened up by the viewer'. In the paintings, human figures are depicted with only one eye or a gaping mouth and holding two fingers up in the air – a salute that became synonymous with the 1989 student uprising. Guan Wei had observed people of all ages making this sign of peace and solidarity across the city prior to the terrible events in Tiananmen Square. His work bears witness to this important social phenomenon and the symbolic power it once held for Beijing's citizens.

ZU: That makes sense. The dark period actually resulted in you producing extraordinary works.

GUAN: There was a sequel to this. Because Geoff Parr thought highly of me, he asked Bernice Murphy and Nicholas Jose to write a letter to the Australia Council. In the letter it said that 'Guan Wei is an important artist who needs to be protected. You should consider providing funding for him to come back to Australia.' And he succeeded – funding was granted by the Australia Council.

ZU: Obtaining a grant from the Australia Council for the Arts was very important.

GUAN: Later on, I found out, this grant was never given to non-Australians. I was an exception. They granted me $10,000. That was a lot of money then. [laughs] The funding was given to the School of Creative Arts at the University of Tasmania for me to make new works.

The second time I arrived in Australia was in August 1990, by invitation. I went to Hobart and concentrated on making new works.

ZU: How long were you there?

GUAN: About a year and a half. During this time, Geoff asked Bernice to take me on. By 1992, the MCA was just being built at its current location. I was the first artist-in-residence.

ZU: Perfect! That's amazing!

GUAN: I didn't really have a job. It was the same time that the MCA was organising the 'Mao Goes Pop' exhibition. I helped them put that together. It went on for another year. Then Liu Pin, my wife, came.

ZU: That would have made life better!

GUAN: Yes. That was what made me stay in Sydney.

As my visa was about to expire, David Williams from the Canberra School of Art at the Australian National University (1993) invited me for an artist-in-residency for half a year.

ZU: How did that happen?

GUAN: It was all through recommendation. [smiles] Australia, like China, has a small circle. They talk to each other and take turns. [laughs]

ZU: It's like a chain.

GUAN: Correct! [laughs]

I had met Gene [Sherman] before I went to Canberra.

ZU: Meeting Gene Sherman was a coincidence, wasn't it?

GUAN: Yes. That was during my free time. When I was in Tasmania, all my other artists friends – Ah Xian, Xiao Xian, Shen Shaomin and Lin Chunyan – lived together in Sydney. I was on my own. They invited me over and I stayed with Ah Xian during the summer holidays. They worked so hard, doing all sorts of manual labour to survive. I said to them that's not the way. Let's go and find gallery dealers.

ZU: Was that at your instigation? That was a great suggestion!

GUAN: Yes, it was. At first, Ah Xian couldn't join us because he had to work. It was just Xiao Xian and I wandering around in Paddington, street by street, door by door, for three days. We approached all kinds of galleries and they gave all sorts of excuses to reject us. One gallery was interested but said they didn't show Asian art, however they said another one down the street might be interested.

ZU: He meant Gene Sherman?

GUAN: That's right. It was called Irving Galleries then. She was interested and asked us to leave our phone numbers. A few days later, she called back. Nick helped us to interpret what she said.

As a result, Gene curated a show for Ah Xian, Xiao Xian and me in 1991. It was our first exhibition, called 'Echoes of China: From Behind the Bamboo Curtain – Three Contemporary Chinese Artists'.

Edmund Capon opened the show for us. It was a great opening. I sold one work at that show.

ZU: That's the way to go!

GUAN: The following year, we had another exhibition 'Orientations – The Emperor's New Clothes' (1992). This time there were more artists, including Shen Shaomin, Xiao Lu, Tang Song and Jia Yong, a seven-artist show. Once more, it turned out that only my work was sold.

In 1993, Gene started to represent me. She and Nick helped me to migrate to Australia as a distinguished artist under the special skill category. I had pretty good luck. [smiles]

> *Guan Wei revealed that his self-portrait for his 2016 Archibald entry 'Plastic surgery' was based on the 887 form he filled when applying for Australian permanent residency. The procedure made a deep impression on him. He said he had to provide a great deal of evidence to prove that he was entitled to the label, 'distinguished'. While waiting for the outcome, he and his wife Liu Pin lived at Bronwyn Thomas's home.*

I rented a studio in Newtown to work. Every two years I had an exhibition at Gene's.

ZU: You also exhibited in some important national shows.

GUAN: Yes. There were opportunities, and important national art competitions.

In 1999, the MCA held my ten-year retrospective exhibition, 'Nesting, or the Art of Idleness 1989–1999'. This confirmed my top position in the Australia art world. I was so lucky. The MCA had never held solo exhibitions. To do it they expanded the fourth floor, moving out the offices, and turned it into an exhibition space. Bernice organised the first exhibition of my works. By the time the exhibition opened, she had left the MCA and Sue Cramer was the curator.

Sherman held my exhibition at her gallery a couple of month after this exhibition. It was sold out before it opened. [laughs]

ZU: Of course! Since then you have continued creating new works.

GUAN: I was really lucky in Australia. I never had to do other work. I was always inside the Australian art circle, part of the mainstream. So I have never stopped. Each year I have a few new series of works.

ZU: What do you think of Australian interpretations of your work? Do they differ from you own ideas?

GUAN: The difference is huge. [laughs]

It is a total misreading. [laughs]

But I think it's wonderful to let them misread.

I have many sinologist friends, such as Geremie Barmé, Nicholas Jose and John Clark. Linda [Jaivin] interviewed me for my exhibition. Because my work always had a long narrow vertical shape, people's analysis was that it was an inheritance of the Chinese scroll painting style, combining traditional and contemporary forms. I told Linda that that wasn't the real reason. I said that when I was teaching at high school, living conditions were difficult and we couldn't afford stretchers. The school had wooden window frames that were pulled out when they changed to aluminum windows frames. When they threw them out, I picked up over a hundred and stored them in my office. I used to stretch canvases over them.

ZU: You developed this style because you painted with them.

GUAN: [laughs] I became accustomed to them, very comfortable with the shape. But there was no intention to reference Chinese tradition.

ZU: Ha ha. What a coincidence. It works perfectly well, though.

GUAN: In 1992, I painted a series, 'Test Tube Baby', in Tasmania, combining folk art with science. I thought it would be an interesting experiment. I was posing the question of whether science could be art. It exhibited as 'Silent Energy' at Museum of Modern Art in Oxford, UK in 1993. When the work was shown in public, people thought I was commenting on China's one-child policy.

ZU: Viewers' interpretations are often different from the artist's.

GUAN: I don't mind what they say. [laughs]

ZU: It's interesting. Westerners' perceptions sometimes encompass their preconceptions. Ambiguity and a sense of black humour feed through their interest in China.

GUAN: [laughs] Not really black humour; maybe grey humour.

I actually analysed myself when I was alone in Tasmania and came up with a perspective. Australia is in the middle between China and the West. So my work is about the integration of the two. The other reason was related to my own background. Because I am a Manchu, I have three elements to my art, that is, humour, knowledge and wisdom.

This conversation with Guan Wei provides a glimpse into his environment while he made art in Australia in the early 1990s. In the years that followed, Guan Wei has been recognised as one of Australia's most celebrated artists. He has continued to make works that traverse Beijing and Sydney in his distinctive style. However, in his speech at the opening of 'Reflection' (2017) at Martin Browne Contemporary, he announced a fourth element to his art-making principles – spirituality.

'The interesting part wasn't simply relating to art, it was relating to China itself'

Conversation with Gene Sherman
16 June 2017 and 8 January 2018

Dr Gene Sherman (b. 1947) grew up in Johannesburg, South Africa. She first arrived in Melbourne in 1964 when her family migrated to Australia. Gene Sherman obtained her PhD in French literature from the University of Sydney while raising her two children. She set out on a journey, dealing in Australian and Asia–Pacific art in pursuit of a newly formed world vision.

Gene Sherman was one of the first commercial gallery dealers who introduced contemporary Chinese art to Australian society. Sherman Galleries (1986–2007) not only raised the profile of contemporary Australian art in the world, in particular in the Asia–Pacific region, but the work also reflected Gene's passion, diligence and dedication.

Although I had often visited the Sherman Galleries because I found the gallery's shows interesting and stimulating, I had never met Gene. In April 2017 I contacted her, expressing my interest in having a conversation with her. I told her about my project. She responded almost immediately and very supportively.

This is a compressed version of two conversations with Gene Sherman that took place on the 16th June 2017 and 8th January 2018 in Paddington, Sydney. During the first visit, Gene gave me a brief account of her background growing up in a Jewish family in Johannesburg. She talked about the intensely political climate rooted in the South African Government's apartheid policy, and the Jewish diaspora with its multiplicity of languages and cultural backgrounds. Her descriptions of African tribal groups and colonial European settlers demonstrated her genuine interest in and observations of all races and cultures – the tapestry of humanity itself.

The dialogue started with Gene's family influences, then focused on her insights on China.

ZU: What recollections of your parents can you share?

SHERMAN: My father was a very vibrant man. He was a man with great vision, had accomplished a great interest in and sense of the world at large. He was a beautiful writer, a beautiful speaker, and intellectual and a persuader. We had many books in our house. He started in journalism, ran an insurance company, and finally became a founding director of a huge financial house. He however wasn't very practical on a day-to-day basis. In the end, he lost everything – moneywise as well as his health. He died at 66.

ZU: That's sad … so young. He definitely passed on his vision and persuasive gifts to you.

SHERMAN: [smiles] I have taken something from him … but I am … much more … detailed! My father didn't focus on the details.

ZU: You learnt …

SHERMAN: … from his mistakes.

> Gene talked about the 1961 Sharpeville Massacre in Johannesburg. To help me understand it, she compared it to the June Fourth Tiananmen Square Massacre in 1989. In my view, her personal experience created an empathy and understanding towards the Chinese artists who came to Sydney post 1989.

She also talked about her father's prediction that the South African Apartheid regime was not going to last, even though most white people thought the system would never end. He told the family that the system wasn't fair, that the government was brutal and near sighted.

He persuaded the whole family, four sisters on the maternal side and five siblings on his side plus children – men with different professions, doctors, businessmen, accountants – all to leave, to emigrate together. Australia was chosen as the family's destination.

She said:
> After Sharpeville, all the families started to arrive in Melbourne [between 1963 and 1966], and the breadwinners found jobs. It wasn't so difficult in those days. We were highly educated and Australia was in need of professional people.

Gene shared with me her first migrant experience when she studied at Melbourne University in 1965.

> I looked the same, but I wasn't the same. I had little by way of cultural connections. I was very different; my accent was different; my experiences were different, and my world-view was very different. I had a very unusual father as well! [I had] grown up in South Africa within a liberal, progressive-thinking family.

Among her stories, one memory particularly interested me. Gene's maternal grandmother, Gita, raised four girls from her two marriages on her own. Both of her husbands died young. Her mother and her three sisters were raised by her grandmother. Gene remembered her grandmother vividly.

SHERMAN: My grandmother raised four girls as a seamstress.

ZU: Wow!

SHERMAN: Yes! She cut patterns and sewed and could make anything.

ZU: Were you close to your grandmother?

SHERMAN: Very! When her girls were all married, in Johannesburg, she lived three months with each daughter.

ZU: Oh, how clever!

SHERMAN: She came with her sewing machine and her sewing basket. When our turn came, I used to prepare by cutting out pictures from magazines, even as a little girl. [smiles] 'I like this dress, Granny, I would like you to make it for me … but I don't like the yellow, I want these sleeves …' [bursts out laughing] I was designing!

ZU: Ha ha!

SHERMAN: My mother would say, 'Don't make her work so hard!' [laughs]

Gene and I had a good long laugh together. In November 2017, Gene, at age of 70, has redirected her focus from contemporary art to the Sherman Centre for Culture and Ideas – establishing Fashion and Architecture Hubs which alternate over a five-year period. I couldn't help but point out the connections between her early experiences with her grandmother and this current exploration. Or was it merely a coincidence?

We had fun together!

ZU: I would have loved that! My great-great-aunt was a sewer and she made me a padded jacket when I was six. It was so precious!

How did art come into it for you?

SHERMAN: There were three connections. I studied art history at university for two years.

My mother's sister was an artist. We used to go to galleries. As children, we used to play in her studio.

And my father started collecting art when he became successful. Many Jewish families collected art – some historical, some contemporary. It's ... one of the things they traditionally do. They like collecting; they like the history. Also, the objects are portable. Jews avoided investing money into huge homes because traditionally they were forced to move from one country to another. They didn't buy yachts. They liked portable assets.

ZU: Aha! I see. No wonder you went into the art world. But how were Asian art and teaching French related?

SHERMAN: I was on the front line, so I knew what was happening.

From the mid-1980s, Australian schools implemented a policy of teaching Asian languages in response to the government agenda of building closer relations with the Asia–Pacific, given the combination of geographic proximity and cultural differences. Gene had to change careers after 17 years of teaching French because it was one of the foreign languages that was losing ground in many schools and universities.

I thought, What I will I do? I'll open a gallery. And because Australia is pivoting to this region and I didn't know the Asia–Pacific region at all – I had been busy with Europe and Africa – I would learn a huge amount.

ZU: That was an insightful vision.

Gene first worked at the Irving Sculpture Gallery in Glebe. She managed the gallery on her own because the director Celia Winter-Irving decided to research a book on Zimbabwean stone sculpture in Africa. On Winter-Irving's return, she asked Gene to take over the gallery. In 1986, Gene and Brian Sherman bought the gallery and moved to the building they owned in Hargrave Street, changing its name to Irving Galleries.

SHERMAN: That was my vision – a gallery focusing on the art of Asia–Pacific and Australia. Unlike my father, of course, I took care of the details. [laughs] I met Nick Jose.

ZU: When was that?

SHERMAN: That was 1988. He was back from China. Actually, he came to me.

One day a man came up the stairs and said to me, 'I want to have a discussion with you about China.' And I said: 'Oh! I'd love to … Do you know China?' So we arranged a time and we had coffee. He brought me papers and catalogues from China and Taiwan. And that was the start of my journey!

ZU: What a perfect timing. What was the discussion?

SHERMAN: I said, 'China? Are you allowed to go there?' [laughs] You know, I had no sense of modern China at all. I went along a very long journey with Nick and Claire [Roberts]. Claire offered to curate a show of Chinese artists, which she did.

In 1991, Gene Sherman and Bill Wright curated the show for Chinese contemporary artists Guan Wei, Ah Xian and Liu Xiaoxian at Irving Galleries: 'Echoes of China from behind the Bamboo Curtain – Three contemporary Chinese Artists'. The following year, 'Orientations – The Emperor's New Clothes' (1992) was curated by Claire Roberts.

ZU: If I could put this into perspective, it seems to me that Nick planted a seed in your mind in 1988. I want to know what exactly was it that interested you?

SHERMAN: Yes, he did. I was very surprised initially as I didn't realise that there was contemporary activity in that part of the world, I didn't know much about China. Coming from South Africa with a focus from my family's perspective on Europe, then on the colonisation of Africa, China felt far away, remote. I suppose my interest wasn't simply in relation to art but in relation to China itself.

The idea of this gap in my knowledge about China bothered me. I started feeling guilty and slightly embarrassed that this huge part of the world was such a blank in my mind.

ZU: I see.

SHERMAN: When I went to study in Paris in 1965, I was there for six months, just before the Cultural Revolution. French students were excitedly running around the university with *Le Livre rouge*, Mao Zedong's *Red Book*. I remember asking 'What is this book?' and they said, 'Oh, it's written by Mao Zedong, the greatest revolutionary. He will change the world …' I thought I'd better check it out. I bought the *Red Book*, I read it in French, and I thought, 'I don't see anything special in it.'

ZU: It didn't speak to you.

SHERMAN: No. It didn't seem important to me. I couldn't see the great importance of the thoughts that were expressed; they seemed simplistic. I decided to let others debate the issues. I was there to learn French, I wanted to master the language.

But the ideas somehow remained with me – Mao Zedong, communism – and when Nick arrived on my doorstep 20 years or so later – I suddenly thought about that *Red Book*. [laughs]

And then I started reading! I read and read as much as I possibly could. I have a huge library of books in translation, fiction, non-fiction on China.

ZU: Now I understand the context.

SHERMAN: Yes, there was definitely a context!

That was before Guan Wei and Ah Xian came to the gallery.

ZU: Again, good timing!

SHERMAN: I saw them come up the stairs in Hargrave Street – three young Chinese men talking in Chinese … I just knew they were artists.

ZU: Ha ha. They had the look.

SHERMAN: You know, I had been working with artists for a long time. I had made it my policy not to see artists who came into the gallery. Otherwise you never had a minute of peace. What we did – Bill Wright, my curatorial director, and I – was that if artists wanted to show us their work, we encouraged them to send slides and once a month, we set aside a morning, opened the cupboard with the CVs and slides and we went through everything.

> *Bill Wright AM (1937–2014) was an artist and curator. He was assistant director at the Art Gallery of NSW from 1982 to 1991, artistic director of the 4th Biennale of Sydney in 1982 and curatorial director at Sydney's Sherman Galleries from 1992 to 2005.*

So, as they came upstairs, I thought I'd say 'I'm not able to …!' but they were looking at me and speaking Chinese.

ZU: Oh dear!

SHERMAN: ... I didn't know what to say ... [laughs]

I said to them, 'Does anyone speak English?'. Only Xiaoxian said, 'I do a little.'

I said, 'Listen, are you artists?'

'Yes!'

I said, 'I don't do this normally. Where are you from?'

And they said, 'China.'

I asked, 'How did you get here?'

They said, 'It's a long story.'

I said, 'Look, I've got ten minutes. Have you got work here to show me?' and they said, 'YES!!'

And I said, 'Where is it?'

'Downstairs!' [laughs] And three of them ran downstairs. [laughs]

And they laid their work out ... [pause] and ... I had never seen anything like it before. It was completely different.

The most interesting one for me at that time was definitely Guan Wei. The symbolic little figures attracted and perplexed me. I couldn't work out what they meant because I didn't have the references or understand the context well enough.

ZU: He had stories to tell ...

SHERMAN: Yes, stories I couldn't find a way into. So, I brought Nick back to translate for us.

I think there was kind of playfulness into it, a whimsical feeling, despite the fact that the artist's aesthetic in the earlier days was very grey and sombre. I felt intuitively that there was a serious intent and yet the atmosphere was happy at the same time.

ZU: I assume your observations were on the mark.

SHERMAN: That's how Guan Wei really was. He laughed a lot. At the beginning, I couldn't understand what was funny. Remember we had Nick translate for us. I saw he was laughing but I couldn't see the funny side of it. Later I understood that his laughter helped get rid of nervousness. The laughter also had roots in his character, in the [Manchu] Bannermen culture of his ancestors and in the Beijing in which he had been raised. He definitely had had a very hard time, like all of them.

ZU: Yes, of course.

SHERMAN: During that period, he had had a painful – beyond painful – time, and yet his attitude to life was to keep it light. Still is, today!

ZU: That's true.

SHERMAN: Those are the two sides of his laughter.

> *Gene recounted the letters she and Nicholas Jose wrote and persuaded others to write to the Department of Immigration to help Guan Wei stay in Australia.*
>
> *Gene praised Guan Wei's wife, Liu Pin, who joined him in Sydney two years later, for her determination and ability to learn English. Very quickly, Liu Pin was translating for hm.*

ZU: You were the one of very first commercial galleries to show Chinese artists. Did you pay much attention to curating these exhibitions?

SHERMAN: Yes. I was one of the few dealer galleries with that interest and eventually that background. In a way my heart was more on the curatorial side rather than the selling side, but I was selling by accident. I didn't mind the marketing side, you know. And it was very helpful to the artists.

However, if only I had been selling, I wouldn't have lasted. It would never have been enough for me.

ZU: I understand that. Your vision went a lot further than instant gain.

SHERMAN: I saw the importance of China very early. I was interested in broader horizons beyond art itself. Australia is in the Asia–Pacific region. People asked me how did you know to leave South Africa in 1964? I responded how did you not know? Some people don't want to see what is clearly in front of them.

So that was that. With regards to relationships with artists, I tried to see the relationship from their point of view, which many dealers find difficult. They see their galleries from the clients' point of view or from their own point of view.

ZU: I often wondered how you were able to bring the top artists to your gallery. As a case in point, I want to talk to you about Ai Weiwei.

SHERMAN: I think you know, that once you are in a circle with curators and museum directors, you share their interests. It was such a small circle then. I knew what was happening and I got to meet the artists.

Ai Weiwei was involved with Charles Merewether's Biennale in 2006. I had always offered our Sherman Visual Arts Residency cottage to the Biennale of Sydney, the University of Sydney, the MCA, depending on the schedule, to help with the cost of art world accommodation. With regard to the Sydney Biennale, I requested Asian artists in particularly, and we hosted Song Dong, Yin Xiuzhen, Gu Wenda, and many others stayed at our residency at some point.

I said to Charles Merewether, before the announcement of Biennale in 2004 when he was putting the invited artists list together. I said, when you put together your Asian artists list – I was assuming there would be some – it doesn't matter if they are Chinese or not, do let me know because I will offer a little freight money. It was around $6000, which I offered every two years, depending on the work in the Biennale, and the accommodation.

Gene explained that after some back and forth with Charles Merewether, Ai Weiwei came with his wife Lu Qing, and stayed for three weeks.

Ai's installation work, 'World Map', was exhibited at the 15th Biennale of Sydney (2006) at the Art Gallery of NSW.

We had breakfast, lunch and dinner with them. He wasn't famous then.

ZU: I see. That's how you got to know each other.

SHERMAN: Yes. And at that stage I really knew I was going to do SCAF, our Contemporary Art Foundation. Nobody else knew. I said to him, 'I want you to promise to keep it quiet, but I want you to be the inaugural artist.' He said: 'I promise.' And he came. [smiles]

'Ai Weiwei: Under Construction' (2008), curated by Dr Charles Merewether, was the inaugural exhibition of the Sherman Contemporary Art Foundation (SCAF). It was a two-site overview of Ai Weiwei's work initiated by the Foundation and shown at both the Paddington Foundation and Campbelltown Arts Centre.

So making connections wasn't difficult for me to do. The group was so small, we all knew one another. According to each one's skills and interests, different people contributed different things. The goal was, however, always the same.

ZU: Exactly.

SHERMAN: How to get these artists to show, become known, and integrated to some extent into the mainstream commercially, and to encourage them to speak English. And papers, visas, they have to have proper papers … there were so many facets to it.

Some of the people who were involved are no longer alive, for example Bronwyn Thomas. She was very important. A small group of people picked up on these waves of information, each in his or her own way, but shared as well.

Although Dr Gene Sherman has refocused her visions away from contemporary art, the exhibitions that Sherman held for Chinese artists from the early 1990s into the second millennium provided information and insights for Australians to see contemporary China. Sherman's vision and interpretation not only captured important changes in China but also influenced the way many people viewed China through its art.

A creative period that produced great artists

Conversation with Nicholas Jose
18 May 2017

Professor Nicholas (Nick) Jose was born in London in 1952 to Australian parents. He is an author, academic and former diplomat. In the 1980s, he worked in China teaching English and Australian literature at Beijing Foreign Studies University (1986) and East China Normal University (1987). Chinese friends call him Zhou Si. From 1987 to 1990, Nick took up the position of cultural counsellor at the Australian Embassy in Beijing. After returning to Australia from China, he worked as a writer and arts consultant before resuming his teaching career. At the time of writing, he is a professor of English and Creative Writing in the School of Humanities, University of Adelaide.

The depth of Nick's experience in China makes him one of Australia's most recognised commentators on contemporary Chinese culture, and on political and cultural relations between China, Australia and the world. His observations about China's history and directions influence Australian decision makers, especially those interested in building a deeper understanding of contemporary China.

Nick has written widely about contemporary China. His creative work includes novels and short stories set between China and Australia but the focus of his scholarship is not only literary. His expertise also crosses over into the visual arts. Nick was a curatorial adviser to Sydney's Museum of Contemporary Art for its major 1993 international exhibition of contemporary Chinese artists, 'Mao Goes Pop: China Post 1989'. The show explored the disillusionment and cynicism in Chinese society in the post-Tiananmen era. It was a manifestation of Chinese avant-garde artists' use of the power of art as a force for social change. In 1995, Nick was also an adviser for 'ARTTAIWAN', the first major exhibition by contemporary Taiwanese artists in Australia. The exhibition explored the complex political issues faced by the country in the early 1990s and engaged with emerging social and cultural identities.

Nicholas Jose has been involved with Chinese art and Chinese artists since the 1980s. I met Nick when Claire Roberts introduced us at an exhibition opening in 2010.

Nick was in Sydney to deliver a public lecture, 'Gifts from China', at Sydney University's Confucius Institute on 17 May. Our dialogue took place on the following day at the Western Sydney University Vice-Chancellor's office at Grosvenor Place, The Rocks. Nick came by bus. He wore a checked white shirt, a backpack and a warm intelligent smile behind his spectacles. We took the lift to the office on Level 31. Our conversation started naturally.

ZU: I am so sorry I missed your lecture last night. Your title was intriguing. What were the gifts from China?

JOSE: I asked the question 'What has China given me?' First, more than thirty years of involvement with China. Then I asked what China has given Australia. The answer for me is really ideas and people.

ZU: That's very important.

JOSE: One of the ideas is a sense of change, the possibility of change. And I take that back to the *I Ching*, the Book of Changes – everything is always changing.

ZU: That's the law of nature.

JOSE: The other change was to my sense of scale, of time and space. It's made me see Australia differently.

ZU: I suppose that you were interested in China at a very young age because of the family influence?

JOSE: Let me explain. People often ask me how I came to be interested in China. Although Australia and China established diplomatic relations in 1972, China was relatively closed and it was unusual for Australians to be very interested in China. Unlike some of my contemporaries, I didn't study Chinese as an undergraduate at ANU (Australian National University). It was later, when I was at Oxford and thinking about returning to Australia, that I began to think more about China, and Australia's future relationship with China. I had an American friend at Oxford who had grown up in Japan. He spoke Japanese and studied classical Chinese but he had never been to China. In the 1970s, few Westerners visited China, but he always dreamed of going there. He said to me, 'If you really want to be a citizen of the world, you must learn Chinese.' I was studying English literature at that time. But I said, 'OK, I can see that.'

ZU: What did you see?

JOSE: I thought from an Australian perspective, in the future, China would probably be important, so when I came back from Oxford in 1978, I enrolled the next year in a Chinese course in Canberra. Just as a hobby ... Then I got hooked by the language. Wonderful teachers! Incredible teachers!

> *Nick was a lecturer, teaching literature at the ANU while studying Chinese part time at the Canberra College of Advanced Education.*

I went to China in 1983 with a student group from what is now the University of Canberra. They organised a four-week study tour for us to Beijing Erwai [Beijing International Studies University]. That was a wonderful experience.

ZU: How much of China did you see?

JOSE: Definitely not everything. In Beijing, we went to the Great Wall. We went to Chengde. At the end, we went to Shanghai and Suzhou. That was all.

In 1983, life in China seemed simple to me as a visitor and change was in the air. You could see in 1983 that China was opening up and moving forward.

ZU: Life was hard but it was a good hardship.

JOSE: Yes. Very optimistic and opening up. So, memorable meetings with people, intense conversations ...

ZU: Was the positive experience you had what took you back a second time?

JOSE: Yes. I decided that I must go back for a longer period, so I arranged to go and teach. In 1986, I taught English at Beiwai [Beijing Foreign Languages Institute].

ZU: English literature?

JOSE: English literature and also Australian literature.

ZU: Really?

JOSE: Yes. Because Beiwai had an Australian studies centre at that time, one of the first in China. You probably know the story. There was a group of scholars who came to study at Sydney University in 1979. They were nicknamed the Gang of Nine.

> *In 1979, some of the first postgraduate students to leave China under Deng Xiaoping's reforms enrolled at the University of Sydney. The 'Gang of Nine' returned to China in 1981 and took up senior positions at Chinese universities. One of them recounted his experiences.*
>
> When I learned I would go to Australia ... I rushed to the library to read books on it – that it was in the South Pacific, and that merino wool came from there.

Many of them studied literature. When they went back, they set up Australian studies centres. They are mostly still going, one at Beiwai, and one at Huadong Shida [East China Normal University] in Shanghai. There are now 35 Australian studies centres in China.

ZU: What did you teach for Australian literature?

JOSE: I probably started with short stories from the colonial period – Henry Lawson – then somewhere we would study Patrick White. It largely started with the 20th century, including some poetry. It was an undergraduate course with a small group of students. I also taught Introduction to English

Literature to first years. That was a big group. I'm still in touch with some of those students, thirty years later.

ZU: Introduction to English Literature would probably have been more familiar for the Chinese students. They wouldn't have had any idea what Australian literature was about. What you taught them was very special. When I was at university in the 1980s, I had no idea what Australia was like.

Did you first hear about China from your grandfather?

JOSE: My father's father was born in China, in Ningbo, but he left as a small child. So it was my great-great-grandfather – three generations back – who lived in China and spoke Chinese.

ZU: You probably never met him.

JOSE: I was four years old when he died. I have memories of him, and he had things from China in his house which he gave to my grandfather. I remember those things.

ZU: What kind of things?

JOSE: *Duilian* [handwritten couplets written on scrolls or displayed on doorways] and some other artifacts, including a pipe, a passport and a bible. But also, my great-grandfather told a lot of stories about life in China to his son, my grandfather, and my grandmother, which they told me. So I heard quite a lot about China as a child. But I didn't really connect with it until I later got interested in China myself.

ZU: It sounds like a seed finally sprouted.

JOSE: Let me tell you something interesting. My great-grandfather, when he was in China, was very interested in photography. That was in the 1890s.

ZU: Do you mean glass plate?

I gestured, describing the size of a big box camera.

JOSE: Yes, the old-fashioned kind. [laughs] He took lots of photographs. He was very interested in Chinese folk art, papercuts and puppets.

ZU: Ha ha. That's what I do today, and shadow play. I must be living in the wrong time. What did he do with his photographs?

JOSE: When he came to Adelaide in the early 20th century, he gave public lectures about Chinese art.

ZU: Wow! That's wonderful. Where can I find them?

JOSE: You can't. There's no record. He gave Chinese art lectures in art institutes. And some Australian artists heard these lectures. One of them was Margaret Preston. We have some colour slides from China he brought back to illustrate the papercuts, masks and other things he showed in these lectures.

ZU: Indeed. I can imagine the images from what you've just described.

JOSE: So, that's quite an interesting connection to Australia through Chinese art. But I have no training in art.

ZU: That's right. I was going to ask, although you don't make art, I believe you made friends with many artists in China.

JOSE: When I went to China in 1986 as a teacher at Beiwai, I already knew there were a lot of creative changes taking place in China. I knew about the 1985 *Xinchao* [85 New Wave], I knew about the writers; the 'misty' poets, *menglong shiren*. So I wanted to meet these people. I had some introductions.

ZU: Were you introduced by Chinese people?

JOSE: Because I came from ANU in Canberra, my friend the scholar Geremie Barmé (Bai Jieming) was one contact, and the writer Linda Jaivin. Linda was a journalist for *Asiaweek*, a news magazine based in Hong Kong. Geremie would visit quite often. Geremie and his colleague John Minford edited an important book called *Seeds of Fire* in 1985, which I had read, and that included contemporary literature and art. In that book you'd find images, for example, by [artists] Ma Desheng, Wang Keping, Ah Xian, Yan Li. In that book, there are Bei Dao's poems, and some essays on politics and society. Wei Jingsheng's writing on the Fifth Modernisation, Democracy, was an important inclusion. It was an influential compilation of new creative expression from the Chinese world.

The four modernisations (agriculture, industry, defence, and science and technology) campaign took place in China soon after the fall of the Gang of Four.

ZU: How did you handle that? Between 1987 and 1990, you were a diplomat at the Australian Embassy in China and you would have been aware that these people were opposing the government.

JOSE: Yes, but I met them in 1986 before I was a diplomat.

ZU: You were free, with no professional obligations then.

JOSE: I was a teacher and a writer, a so-called 'foreign expert'. I wasn't an employee of the Australian government.

ZU: Then things changed?

JOSE: I knew most of my artist and writer friends in Beijing before I worked at the Australian Embassy. That was because I taught in Beijing and in Shanghai in 1986 and 1987. At the end of 1987, I got the job as the cultural counsellor at the embassy.

ZU: Did you stay China during this transition?

JOSE: I returned to Australia for two months for training and to visit cultural institutions in Australia.

I had a meeting at the MCA with the founding directors, Bernice Murphy and Leon Paroissien. I told them there is new art in China that no one in the art world knows about. It's very exciting; it's very important. They were interested. The MCA had started doing international exhibitions that were regional and doing something different. They did one with New Zealand, they did one focusing on East Germany and another on Japan, as I recall.

They were very curious and they said yes, they would be interested to explore an exhibition of new Chinese art as part of their program. In fact, Leon had visited China much earlier, in the period of PM Gough Whitlam, and had a strong commitment to doing projects with China. They said they were interested – keep in touch.

ZU: OK.

JOSE: I started working in the embassy in November 1987. One of the first cultural delegations to come from Australia was an art education delegation in 1988. It consisted of Betty Churcher, who became the director of the National Gallery of Australia in Canberra, but at that time was the director of Art Gallery of Western Australia in Perth. Geoff Parr, who was the head of the art school at Hobart, part of the University of Tasmania, and David Williams who was the head of the Canberra School of Art & Design, affiliated with ANU. Three very influential people came to China for a visit of a couple of weeks. We had an official itinerary – going to different art schools, Meiyuan (Central Academy of Fine Arts), Gongyi Meiyuan (Academy of Arts & Design), and Hangzhou Zhejiang Meiyuan (China Academy of Art).

ZU: Did you take them around?

JOSE: Yes. The Ministry of Culture was the host. But the visitors said, 'We want to see more. We want to see new art.'

ZU: I suppose they meant they had enough of Western art because that's what we were trained in at art school.

JOSE: Yes. They wanted to see unofficial art. So I arranged for them to see it. They met Guan Wei.

ZU: Was this at your apartment?

JOSE: Yes. There was a meeting in my apartment. Artists brought along their work. And the delegation made visits to some of the artists' houses or other small spaces where work was on display, such as the Yinyueting (Beijing Concert Hall).

ZU: Yes, the Yinyueting had some artworks displayed in the foyer. I remember seeing them when I heard Tan Dun perform.

JOSE: Yes. There was some very interesting art there. The French Cultural Centre had an active program and some other embassies had spaces they could make available. Otherwise it was a matter of arranging small temporary exhibitions in the apartments of foreign residents.

ZU: How interesting. I had a show at the French Cultural Centre in early 1988 before I came to Australia.

JOSE: That delegation was important. Geoff Parr, David Williams and Betty Churcher saw a range of art and met artists. Among them were Guan Wei, Ah Xian, Lin Chunyan. The visitors were very excited. They wanted to develop relationships between art schools in China and Australia. Geoff Parr said, 'I want to invite these artists to an artist-in-residence in Hobart as soon as possible.'

ZU: Now I have completed the missing puzzle of how these three artists came to Australia. It was through your introduction.

JOSE: Yes. I introduced them.

ZU: But how did you meet them?

JOSE: Back in 1986, there were a lot of events. I met Mang Ke, the poet, first. Later the poet Yang Lian, and other artists who were part of that group. They are friends of each other. Lin Chunyan had an exhibition – I remember that one clearly – at the Observatory, Jianguomen, where the Red Gate Gallery later was. But in 1986, it was a space where artists could exhibit. There were small groups of people, many of whom had grown up together or were connected in other ways. I met some of them. Some I became more friendly with, partly because of living in Zhongguancun [in Beijing's Haidian district] and teaching at Beiwai. Ah Xian lived next door in Ligong Daxue [Beijing Institute of Technology]. Lin Chunyan lived close by and had a similar family background.

ZU: Were you planning the new China art exhibition at this time?

JOSE: People from that delegation were close friends with the MCA people and I suppose they talked to each other when they got back to Australia.

ZU: That makes sense. It sounds like an organic development.

JOSE: In 1988, people from the MCA came to China to visit and to meet with artists. Then, the 'Avant-Garde' exhibition happened in February 1989. That got media attention around the world. I knew Hou Hanru, Li Xianting and other people who were involved in that exhibition. That exhibition was amazing. It was a very good group exhibition. I saw the works in the exhibition and I liked some of the works very much. I also met some of the artists.

ZU: I remember I was as shocked as everyone else at the time when the Chinese officials closed the exhibition on the same day it opened.

JOSE: As you know, it closed, and there was no plan about what would happen to those works at the end of the exhibition. So, very quickly, Johnson Chang from Hanart [TZ Gallery] in Hong Kong, who had already been exhibiting works from The Stars Group and other contemporary artists from Taiwan, such as Zhu Ming, Yu Peng, Cheng Tsai-tung – various Taiwanese artists. He was already developing an interest in new art from the Chinese world.

ZU: I am not very familiar with Taiwanese artists because at the time I lived in China, we had no connection with Taiwan.

JOSE: Part of the background is that the Taiwanese artists had done quite a lot of political art in the 1980s because of martial law. They had a period of quite violent protest and demonstrations, and produced this kind of political art in the 1980s. This very small gallery in Hong Kong, Hanart, started to promote these artists.

Johnson Chang is a brilliant person, a writer and critic as well as a gallery director. He quickly contacted the organisers of the 1989 exhibition and said, 'I want to take as much as possible of this art to Hong Kong.' To get together that type of money and support, he needed international partners. I introduced him to the MCA. The exhibition began in Hong Kong under the title 'China's New Art: Post-1989'. It came to Australia in a slightly different form, managed by Hanart and the MCA, with Li Xianting credited as curator. In Sydney and on tour in Australia it was called 'Mao Goes Pop'.

ZU: I see. I read the Hong Kong catalogue in Chinese. Who gave it the title, 'Mao Goes Pop'?

JOSE: I think it was the marketing department in MCA. They thought that would work.

ZU: Did you go to the opening? How was it?

JOSE: Yes. It was incredibly successful! It is probably the best exhibition the MCA has ever had in terms of attendance and feedback. It was the first time in the world that this art had been seen outside China and Hong Kong. It was very significant.

In Australia, young people, including many art students and high school students, copied it. The work at ArtExpress [NSW high school art exhibition] in the years following copied a lot from that exhibition.

ZU: Well! That's wonderful, isn't it!

JOSE: Yes. It is wonderful.

The Sydney exhibition was slightly different from Hong Kong, as I've mentioned. Some of the content was different.

Because what happened between February 1989 when 'China Avant-Garde' was on show briefly in Beijing and 1993 in Sydney was June Fourth. And what June Fourth meant for Australia is that a lot of people came here. Some of them were artists.

The MCA show included Guan Wei, Ah Xian, Wang Youshen, Xiao Lu and Tang Song as artists who had some connection with Australia.

ZU: Were you personally involved in selecting the artists and works?

JOSE: My role was curatorial adviser. The MCA made certain decisions, partly to do with the space and what was available. Getting the works from Beijing to Hong Kong was already difficult; getting them from Hong Kong to Sydney was another difficult exercise.

ZU: Do you mean difficulties in terms of time and expense, or something else?

JOSE: Time, expense, availability, the condition of the work, the size and scale of the work – all of those things.

In parallel to the MCA's interest was the exhibition that Claire [Roberts] was developing for the Queensland Art Gallery which was shown at the Art Gallery of NSW in 1992, 'New Art from China'. That was happening around the same time. It was the pioneering exhibition of contemporary Chinese art in Australia, a real first. Claire had major artists in her show who were in the Beijing show, notably Xu Bing and Fang Lijun. 'Mao Goes Pop' followed on a larger scale.

ZU: Yes, indeed. But the two shows were not a collaboration.

JOSE: No. We talked about it, but 'Mao Goes Pop' was not my project. It was the MCA's.

'New Art from China' was Claire's project with the Queensland Art Gallery as the first partner, and the Art Gallery of NSW as the second partner. In her exhibition she was interested partly in the continuation of traditional Chinese elements – woodblock printing, brush-and-ink paintings.

ZU: I guess Claire also brought in her own expertise and interest in Chinese painting. What is your interest in Chinese art?

JOSE: Yes. That's her expertise. Whereas 'Mao Goes Pop' was coming out of the February 1989 show from Beijing. It followed more closely Li Xianting's analysis of contemporary Chinese art. A big part of it focused on the political pop movement of Li Shan, Wang Guangyi, Liu Wei and others.

In March 1992, Li Xianting's essay 'Major Trends in the Development of Contemporary Chinese Art', Nick's essay 'Towards the World: China's new art, 1989–93' and articles by Yi Ying, Geremie Barmé, Liao Wen, Fei Dawei and others were published in the 'China's New Art, Post-1989' exhibition catalogue, Hanart TZ Gallery, Hong Kong.

ZU: When you talk about a political approach, in my view, all art is political because it takes a stand. However, some artists say their work is misinterpreted while others are actually happy about the mismatch between the artist's intention and public reaction. What is your view?

JOSE: Ultimately, the interpretation is not for the artist, it's for the viewer. No one interpretation can be correct, regardless of the artist's intention. But it must of course be based on knowledge and understanding. One of the strange things that happens when Chinese art goes to international spaces is that people with no knowledge will interpret it. They may get it wrong. But generally speaking, I think art is subtle, and art can be ambiguous; it doesn't have one simple meaning usually.

ZU: I agree. Are you an art collector?

JOSE: No. Only if I like something. Claire and I gave the Queensland Gallery some works we had that we wanted to be in a public collection – works by Fang Lijun, Zhang Xiaogang, Yu Youhan and others.

ZU: My goodness. That's very generous of you!

JOSE: Also, Liu Xiaodong, a wonderful painting called 'Smoker' that he gave to me in 1989 and I passed on to the Queensland Art Gallery because I promised the artist it would go to a public collection.

Nick had listed the best known contemporary Chinese artists whose paintings are now worth a fortune. At the time, of course, there was no market for them.

ZU: What is your view of current contemporary Chinese art?

JOSE: Look, I'm not really up to date on Chinese art. I don't follow contemporary art in China closely.

ZU: Are you saying the engagement or the involvement you had with Chinese art was because of the relationship you had with artists?

JOSE: I believe that the 1980s was a very creative period in China and it produced great artists. That whole generation had very interesting artists. But I don't think that continues. That was a historical moment. That's my view.

ZU: Do you think that because you experienced that special period, a most turbulent, traumatic time in China, you understood the context of the work, you saw things behind the art?

JOSE: Yes. I think so. I understand the context, but it was also my own life experience [putting his hand on his heart], so I related to it. And now there is a new generation, with a very different life experience.

I think art moves around. Good art is not everywhere all the time. Different countries produce good art at different times. If you look at Australian art, you can see the 1940s was a very strong period, but it doesn't continue necessarily. Look at Aboriginal art, in the early 1970s. It was very important, communicating very deep things in new ways for the first time, but that changes. It's impossible to keep up that level of creative originality.

And I think art in China is the same. There was a period of real creative energy in the 1980s.

ZU: Do you think it's possible to sustain Chinese art and tradition? When dealing with change, what has been retained from the Chinese tradition?

JOSE: Well ... [pauses, searching for the right words] for me it's personal. I'm connected to China in so many ways, so I continue that involvement but in a really personal way. So, I do some things. I organise some events and discussions. I take students to China. I follow some things but I don't ... keep up with everything.

ZU: I don't think you need to. [smiles] It's not your job.

JOSE: [laughs] It's not possible.

ZU: It's not your responsibility either. Like me – I make art because I want to, not because I have to. It's because of this that I feel some contemporary work, not only in China but in Australia too, lacks sincerity.

JOSE: I think I understand that.

ZU: But I am sure you will never lose your interest in China.

JOSE: No. There are always good things coming from China. Last week, I was in Guangzhou meeting with the Chinese writers at the China–Australia Literary Forum. I met a very interesting young woman poet from Guangzhou. I read her work and heard her talk. It was something new for me. She was a factory worker, *mingong* [migrant worker], and she has become a very good poet – writing about the factory.

ZU: Do you think your China experience has influenced your teaching and writing style?

JOSE: Definitely! No question there. Not only my writing style, but also what I am interested in.

ZU: ... and your way of thinking?

JOSE: Yes. I am very interested in connections between different people, and the flow between people and from one place to the other, across time.

ZU: This doesn't sound much like Western dualism.

JOSE: Totally the opposite of it, and it's not linear either.

ZU: When you visit China now, do you miss the times that have passed?

JOSE: No, you can't. There's no point. Change happens ...

Our conversation concluded naturally, as it had begun. There was so much to contemplate and reflect on. Meeting Nicholas Jose has changed this book. I came to realise that what I am writing about concerns friendship, love, humanity and hope.

He left me with a sense of peace and kindness, but also a touch of hopelessness about the impossibility of keeping up with things.

Is it possible to play?

Conversation with Liu Xiaoxian
10 January 2018

Liu Xiaoxian was born in Beijing in 1963. He studied optical engineering at the Beijing Institute of Technology (1981–85). Influenced by his brother Ah Xian and his artist friends, he made a career change and started taking photographs as a way of making art. In 1990, after the June Fourth Incident – the Tiananmen Square Massacre – he came to Australia with other two artists Ah Xian and Wang Youshen, joining an art exhibition called 'The International Art Festival of New Music and Visual Art' at the Art Gallery of NSW. In turn, he joined the new generation of Chinese diaspora seeking new opportunities and freedom in his art career.

Between 1999 and 2002, Liu Xiaoxian undertook a Master of Arts in photomedia at the Sydney College of the Arts. SCA also provided him with the opportunity to explore other media such as clay and glass.

Liu is recognised as one of Australia's leading photographers and contemporary artists. Although many of his works play out the life he experienced as an 'adopted' Australian, he acknowledges that he has never renounced his deep-rooted Chinese identity. His works contemplate the differences as well as the commonalities between China and the West on issues such as culture, tradition, politics, religion, identity and gender. The juxtaposition of placement and misplacement expressed in his work could perhaps be perceived as an expression of the migrant experience.

I explained to Liu that I was fascinated by his way of intermeshing images of China and Australia and that I would like to have a conversation with him. He invited me to his home in Kingsgrove, Sydney. As he invited me to sit on a Qing style wooden table, I was struck by the arrangement of his lounge room, with its antiques and collectables bought from auction houses, Chinese antique furniture and a huge pile of his two children's plastic toys.

I started with some questions about photography.

ZU: I would like to start by talking about your creation with photomedia.

LIU: In the beginning, my work was photography. Then I tried to change photography's traditional form of presentation. I worked in the darkroom using only photographic techniques. Back then there was no digital processing available anyway.

ZU: Why did you choose photography as your art form?

LIU: It was influenced by my brother [Ah Xian]. He was a painter and interested in painting. But he had a camera, a Minolta 700. He said to me, 'Take it and use it.'

ZU: So you took it and made great use of it.

LIU: He suggested that I could take photos of his artist friends. So, from 1987 to 1989, I took many photos of artists, and portraits of people, mostly in black and white. I often used partial hand-colouring techniques to touch up silver gelatin prints, or using chemicals to make monochrome prints or combinations of both. I made a series called 'The Sound of Silence' by taking photos covering 360° horizontally and 180° vertically of a scene (normally a spot in the Forbidden City or the Summer Palace, etc.). Later on, after June 1989

I created some surrealist style photographic works such as 'Photo', 'Lock', etc. 'Lock' depicts a man within a photo-frame suffering from sewing his own lips and eyelids with a threaded needle.

I came to Sydney in September 1990 and lived with a few other Chinese artists in a suburban house in Enmore. But one day the house was broken into and all my cameras got stolen …

ZU: Oh. That's a shame. Then again, do you actually use a camera in creating your artworks?

LIU: Yes I do, but not directly. Photography is a medium to express my artistic ideas.

ZU: I have this idea that a photograph is a picture taken by a camera in real time but your work definitely is something else. Tell me your ideas about reality.

LIU: Reality can be important, but sometimes it is not. For example, in the surrealist style works I showed you, the subject in the photograph reaches his hand out of the picture to tear off the photo itself, exposing his body. It was originally a male face but it reveals a female body after the stripping off.

ZU: I see. You create something realistic that corresponds to your inner vision. In this, were you following the theories of Freud or the Chinese concepts of yin and yang?

LIU: I wasn't thinking of any theory. I like drama and the work is playful and visually challenging.

ZU: Hmmm …

LIU: I just use the reality I see. Take my work 'Home–London' (2002–03) for example, it was manipulated but I wanted people to feel that the photo was taken at that place. In reality, it is impossible to take a family photo by inserting a large canvas backdrop in between the Royal Army's changing of the guard ceremony, right in front of Buckingham Palace. It's not possible, even for a second. I try to realise the impossible.

ZU: The work becomes reality. The obvious manipulation presents an absurd condition. So, what was the concept behind that work?

LIU: Although I live in Sydney, I don't feel that I am settling down. Home is neither here nor there. And there's another home, and that's my old home back in China. When I realised that I couldn't be in two places at the same time, I tried to make it happen in images. In the old days, people would take a photo in front of a painted backdrop to fulfil their dream of visiting somewhere they may never been. So I took photos of Chinese families in front of a painted Chinese scene to represent my idea of a Chinese home. The whole set was taken in a larger and real 'backdrop' to represent my concept of current living home in the Western world. I wanted to put my two homes together.

The concept is as simple as the food I used to eat, the old friends I used to see. But they are not as easily accessible as they were when I am not in China.

ZU: Yours are very simple ideas.

LIU: Yes, they are. Most of works came from personal experience in my life.

ZU: When the 'Home' series was shown in public, it appeared that there were many ways to interpret the work. For example, the colours you used, the way people dressed and posed for you suggested something else. Did you expect that?

LIU: I asked my friends and their families to pose for me. I explained that I was making an artwork with their images. I made a time to visit them and they pose for me so that I could take the shots. It was all done in these people's home – the front yard or backyard – but I superimposed them to be all around the world. The series included Rome, London, Paris and Australia.

I like making work that has subtlety because it encourages viewers to interpret them in many ways. You can't stop people from seeing different things in the work because each one of them has different life experiences.

ZU: It seems many people enjoyed your optical tricks.

Photography had changed in the past 30 years. How has it changed your work and in what ways have you adapted to the changes?

LIU: The biggest change was when digital imaging replaced traditional chemical-based photography. When I made the 'Home–London' work, the original photo was taken with film, then manipulated on a computer. Now, even the original photos are digital images. It won't ever go back to the old way of doing things.

ZU: When digital cameras started to replace film cameras, a lot of professional photographers felt challenged. Many of the techniques that were difficult to master or achieve with traditional photography were a lot easier with computers.

Your early work 'My Other Lives' (1999) reflected this transition in technology. It's also about the transformation in your Chinese–Australian experience.

In 'My Other Lives' (1999), Liu photographed and superimposed himself as different characters into photos from his collection of 19th century Australian family albums.

LIU: All my works are related to my personal experience. I have collected many old photographs, though in my collection, I haven't come across one Chinese in a Victorian stereographe.

ZU: The way you used photographs to recapture Chinese people playing an important part in Australian culture was very effective. It reminds viewers to reexamine truths that have been overlooked.

LIU: I borrowed the idea of using the differences in perspective that you find in old 3D photography [stereograph] methods and put myself into one of the two images. So it utilises the formation of stereograph with one photograph, but the identity is changed.

ZU: Was this new concept of differences in perspective intended to change identity?

LIU: That's right, but the differences were subtle. I had to set up the same lighting to shoot my photos so as to get as close as possible to the old photograph. I tried using all type of characters – men, women, old and young.

ZU: What is your identity when you perform these different roles?

LIU: Chinese. It's mainly to make Chinese people appear in that period because they were absent.

Xiaoxian said that he had never appreciated the real beauty of a stereograph until he looked through the viewer and the dual-image format prompted him to use its unique characteristics, to adapt and shift the difference in perspective into an alteration of identity.

ZU: By the year 2000, you made further advances in your digital photomedia skills. 'Our Gods' (2000) was a monumental photographic installation.

LIU: I combined the two images with pixels.

'Our Gods' (2000) is a digitally composed diptych photomontage of two portraits, a representation of the suffering Christ and the laughing Buddha. The Christ was made up of tiny figures of Buddha and the Buddha was formed from tiny images of Christ. There are 22,500 small repeated images of the other, like small pixels to form the large figures. 'Our Gods' is in the Asian Art Collection of the Art Gallery of NSW.

My theory is that by using small things and arranging them in a different configuration, a big picture of something else will emerge. It's also the basis of photography. In traditional photography, it's the silver crystals that create the image. I merely used a small image to replace the silver crystal.

ZU: I see. So, that was the basis of its production. Could you explain the idea behind it?

LIU: This work is a continuation of my Eastern and Western comparative study. It covers not only the similarity and difference between Christianity and Buddhism, but also borrows the Taoist symbol yin and yang, that is, one is within the other and everything is in constant movement. It also reveals the relationship between the macrocosm and microcosm. The idea echoes the famous Song Dynasty poet Su Dongpo's words: 'I don't know the true appearance of Mount Lu because I am on the mountain.'

When you are close to the work, you mainly see the small images. You can't see the big picture clearly. When you step back a certain distance, the big picture becomes clearer. It's the same with a mountain. From a distance you can see the mountain, but when you are on the mountain, you see plants and trees.

This matched my observations when I came in Australia. I recognised the differences between Eastern and Western cultures and made many works that were in response to the similarities and differences between them.

ZU: And you are expressing it through Pop Art.

LIU: Yes. Pop Art has major influence on my art creation. During the 80s when I was still in China, I was first exposed to American Pop Art. A show of Rauschenberg in Beijing in 1985 had a big impact on many young artists. Andy Warhol, Chuck Close and David Hockney all had a certain influence on my artistic formation initially. I started to make large images with smaller photographic panels back then and it became one of my main formulas in making mural-sized artworks. Later, after moving to Australia, I started comparing Chinese images with Australian ones, in different areas naturally. Switching the faces (in 'Our Gods') made it more fun.

ZU: New technology plays an important role in your work. Imagine if you had to create a montage of tens of thousands of images by hand.

LIU: I did works like this when I was in China in 1987. I used small photos of Buddha to compose abstract photographs (a series called 'Diary'). I thought if I could deal with abstract forms, I could make realistic figures too.

ZU: It worked!

Using grids is another element in your work.

LIU: That came from the time I started doing montage. The advantage of montage is that I can use small pieces to make a large work. My way of doing it is to arrange things in a very orderly way – namely side by side, not overlapping. Making grids is a basic way of learning how to draw [copy] a picture more accurately. Using one small image as a basic element in an orderly arrangement in order to make another large image, the border of the small image forms grids naturally. Grids became unavoidable, and so does the repetition.

ZU: That makes the installation easy to follow.

I'd like to ask you about another installation sculpture work, 'The way we eat' (2008–09).

> *'The Way We Eat'* is a long row of Western eating implements and one simple pair of chopsticks. It is in the Asian Art Collection of the Art Gallery of NSW.

LIU: I often visit auction houses as a hobby collector. When I saw that there were so many types of Western cutlery, I became very drawn to it. I bought some, and then I found more and more different types. When I was making this work, I could have used the objects I collected directly, but then the artistic 'language' wouldn't have been as pure. It wouldn't have matched my aesthetic requirements. During that period, my brother Ah Xian went to Jingdezhen to make his series of porcelain busts. [smiles] So I was inspired to make the cutleries in porcelain. Some of my artistic development has been influenced by him.

ZU: But you've never lost your own artistic language.

The way I looked at the installation was as a manifestation of acceptance of cultural differences vs assimilation. It worked really well that half the space was installed with mismatched Western eating utensils, leaving the other half an empty space except the pair of chopsticks. The image is so simple but very strong.

When I say strong, I mean the impression it imparts. The object itself, however, feels very fragile. The sculpture feels like jade.

LIU: I made the set using porcelain with celadon glaze. It's a traditional way of replicating jade. It shows the subtle patterns of the bas-relief on the objects. Celadon is beautiful glaze that creates gentle changes in colour. Lighter on the embossed side and a little bit darker on the deeper side. One intention of making them into porcelain is to eliminate their original functionality simply because they become so fragile that one could only take them as precious items to admire but not to use them. Western people have a tradition of using knife and fork to eat because the food is normally served in large piece, which needs to cut into smaller pieces. Whereas Chinese use chopsticks to eat simply because the food is often cooked in small pieces already. Making them into porcelain not only unifies the material in order to purify the artistic language, but it also utilises the characteristic fragility and beauty of the glaze to glorify them into something much more precious.

ZU: The brittleness of the material and subtle changes on the surface may leave viewers with a subconscious impression that this is a sensitive topic that should be handled with caution.

You repeatedly demonstrate an interest in Western and Eastern cultural differences that cannot be bridged, to my way of understanding. Perhaps these are things that are not capable of being integrated.

LIU: Yes. The clearest expression of this idea was the chess pieces called 'Games'. In different cultures, the rules are different, and because of that, one of the games I created cannot be played. In this 'Game', I combined a board with half Chinese chess and the other half with European chess. The two chess games share many similarities: both European and Chinese chess have 32 pieces (16 on each side); both chessboards consist of the same number of squares, except the Chinese chess has a boundary river in between. The movement of certain pieces are almost the same. For example, the rook in Chinese chess is a chariot which moves in straight lines in any number of steps (vertically and horizontally). The knight in Chinese chess is a horse that also jumps diagonally across two squares. The king in Chinese chess is a general. They move one step at a time and only within a four-square-block. There are only five pawns in Chinese chess and they also move one step at a time. The bishops in Chinese chess are elephants or prime ministers but they can only move four squares diagonally and cannot cross the boundary. It is said that all the versions of chess originated in ancient India. Elephants were not used by Chinese in wars traditionally, so this is one piece of evidence that Chinese chess originated from India. Regardless of the similarities and differences, by putting two half chess games together to make one makes the 'Game' unplayable simply because each side has its own rules. It's just like me moving to Australia. I need to follow the rules here. When driving, for example, it's crucial to keep left side on the road.

Xiaoxian shows me images of three different 'Games' (2008–09), a series of chess sets he's made with different materials. One of the glass chess sets has pieces presented as native species such as platypuses, kookaburras, kangaroos, koalas, wombats and dingoes lined up against introduced species like rabbits, rats, foxes, sheep, cows and horses.

This set is closely related to Australia. One side are all introduced species. On the other side they are all native animals. I used white dots to draw the chessboard, which represents the Australian Aboriginal land. Rabbits and foxes were introduced by Europeans but they did damage to the native animals. In carrying out such practices, humans were trying to play God in manipulating nature. This set was commissioned by the Federation Contemporary Exhibition Melbourne in 2001.

ZU: Has anyone attempted to play this game?

LIU: I play both chess games, namely Chinese chess and European chess. I wanted to have a chess master to play my 'Game' and see if it could be done. I also left a big notebook beside this 'Game' installation in the previous exhibitions as to collecting comments and suggestions in order to make this 'Game' playable. However, after all these efforts, I realised that the Western chess pieces move within the squares whereas Chinese chess pieces move on the lines and cross points. [laughs] The pieces never really meet, they just pass by each other. [laughs] Such an irony!

ZU: They travel alongside one another without crashing. How brilliant is that! [laughs]

Before our conversation ended, I asked about Liu's new work. I was curious to see whether he was continuing to pursue his abiding interest in the cultural differences between West and East. Xiaoxian said that the new pieces he's working on are photographic, but they're not strongly related to his previous subjects. He said that the time when he felt so deeply and strongly about cultural differences may have passed.

'I choose to drift'

Conversation with Ah Xian
21 February 2017

Ah Xian was born in Beijing in 1960. He is a self-taught painter and has worked as a professional artist since the early 1980s. Ah Xian is one of Australia's leading contemporary artists. In Australia he is best known for combining the Western tradition of realistic life-size figurative statues with hand-painted or carved Chinese traditional decorative motifs and patterns imprinted on their bodies. He reinterprets the traditional Chinese art materials of porcelain, cloisonné, bronze, lacquer, scholar rocks, jade and bone inlay to explore notions of identity, diaspora, the human conditions and cultural integration.

I met Ah Xian in August 2016. On one occasion I asked if he would talk to me about his art and he gladly agreed. He invited me to his home on 21 February 2017. There are displays of his bust sculptures on the tables, chairs, fireplace and in the hallway. Outside a museum, these life-size figures seem like family members.

At the beginning, I clarified that I wanted to have an artist-to-artist conversation.

ZU: Let's start with your first Australian experience.

AX: I first visited Australia in early 1989 with Lin Chunyan and Guan Wei. We came for a summer artists' residency at the School of Art, University of Tasmania, in Hobart. We stayed there for a few weeks. After that, we visited Melbourne and Sydney for about ten days before heading back Beijing. The residency was organised by the Australian cultural counsellor to China, Professor Nicholas Jose, together with the director of School of Art, Tasmania University at the time Mr Geoff Parr.

ZU: When did you return to Beijing?

AX: I went back to Beijing in April that year. It was close to *liusi*. Students from Beida [Peking University] and Qinghua [Tsinghua University] took to the streets and, as more and more gathered, the square filled up to demonstrate for democracy. Later on, they started a hunger strike.

> *The June Fourth Incident, or liusi, refers to the Chinese government's use of force to suppress student-led demonstrations in Beijing in 1989. It became known as the Tiananmen Square Massacre.*
>
> *This is the BBC News coverage.*
>
> ***1989: Massacre in Tiananmen Square***
> *Several hundred civilians have been shot dead by the Chinese army during a bloody military operation to crush a democratic protest in Peking's (Beijing's) Tiananmen Square.*
>
> *Tanks rumbled through the capital's streets late on 3 June as the army moved into the square from several directions, randomly firing on unarmed protesters.*
>
> *The injured were rushed to hospital on bicycle rickshaws by frantic residents shocked by the army's sudden and extreme response to the peaceful mass protest. Demonstrators, mainly students, had occupied the square for seven weeks, refusing to move until their demands for democratic reform were met.*

I was there. On the night of 3 June, I was around Muxudi, Chang'an Avenue. I saw the violent military trucks and tanks crush through towards Tiananmen Square ...

ZU: You went back at a very intense time in Beijing. I remember it clearly. I was living in Sydney but I watched the news of the students' movement every day. I was so scared and worried. I had friends at Beijing University, Tsinghua University, and Central Academy of Fine Arts (CAFA) who joined the protest. My friends from the CAFA sculpture department created the Statue of Liberty for Tiananmen Square. At the beginning there was hope. Then it all fell apart. I felt so desperate. The tragedy was unspeakable.

When did you come back to Australia?

AX: I returned to Australia in 1990. In late 1989 I met Mr Roger Woodward, the well-known Australian pianist, who was based in London during his visit to Beijing. It was also through an introduction by Professor Nicholas Jose. Mr Woodward invited me, my brother Xiaoxian and another artist friend Wang Youshen to participate in a festival he had organised. It was the Sydney Spring International Festival of New Music. Because he invited us that year, the name of the event was changed to The International Festival of New Music and Visual Arts. They added 'the visual arts' just for us. We had a small show in the foyer of the Art Gallery of NSW.

I had already decided not to return to Beijing but to stay in Sydney with Xiaoxian. We were determined that wherever we went, we would not be returning to China at that dark time. I was going back on my word. After I returned to Beijing from

Hobart, I told many friends that although Australia was great and beautiful, China was my homeland. So even if I went abroad again, I would be back. But, not after June Fourth!

ZU: It changed your view completely.

What was the most difficult thing after you decided to live in Sydney?

AX: The biggest difficulty was to make a living from empty hands. When we left home, Xiaoxian and I only had US$200 and our luggage with a few clothes in it. That's all we had.

ZU: While you were settling in Sydney, your art making had also went through a transformation. How did the transition from painting to sculpture come about?

AX: I did some sculptural works when I was in China. For example, I worked with some used timber slabs that already had a shape. I did some simple work to turn them into something else. I began to work mainly in sculpture a couple of years after I came to Sydney. I've always been interested in realistic figurative works, especially photorealistic effects. At first I worked with plaster. But I soon found that the material itself had a cheap feeling, and yet it wasn't durable. It didn't have the necessary quality for an art object.

I was searching for something similar that was white, good for shaping, fine, and had a more lasting value. It came to me in a flash. I realised porcelain had all these qualities ... However, although I had the idea, I neither knew how to realise a realistic sculpture, nor the process of working in porcelain. I had to work six days a week as a house painter to make a living. But on the weekend or after work, I started to try things out while reading books and asking around to learn the necessary moulding and sculptural skills.

The house we rented in Canterbury had a tin shed in the backyard that I used as my 'studio'. I tried to make objects with porcelain. At first, I couldn't master moulding, so the shapes were often distorted. I kept learning and experimenting. I made hands, feet and faces – up to the neck, no shoulders at the very beginning. I made about 20–30 pieces.

> *Ah Xian showed me a sculpture he made in 1995. It's a figure of his artist friend Guo Jian. They used to work together as house painters to support themselves.*

ZU: I personally quite like the imperfect shapes. To me, I guess, the organic form often exposes a strong presence of the artist.

But of course, you perfected them very quickly.

AX: I participated in the 'In & Out' [Contemporary Art from China and Australia] exhibition at RMIT Gallery in November 1997. At the exhibition, I met the gallery director Suzanne Davies and her husband, Professor Richard Dunn, Dean of Sydney College of the Arts. We became good friends. Richard saw the porcelain work I had produced in my tin shed. He really liked them and invited me to Sydney College of the Arts for an artist-in-residency program. They had just moved from the old campus in Balmain to Rozelle. The new campus of SCA was historical and great. I was offered an individual studio space at the ceramic faculty. They had a number of kilns and a main workshop. It was so handy for me to be working there. I had a one-year (1998) artist-in-residency at SCA where I worked with porcelain.

ZU: What was the outcome?

AX: After a year, I had made about 12 porcelain pieces. With these works, I entered the Third Asia–Pacific Triennial (APT) in 1999. At the end of 1998, I applied for an Australia Council Grant. I had tried unsuccessfully a couple of times before, with different works. But this time, with the new work, I got the grant. With the $20,000 grant, I went to Jingdezhen in early 1999, stayed there for almost a year and made about 40 pieces of porcelain sculpture.

ZU: Who nominated you for APT?

AX: Ms Claire Roberts recommended me for APT. Mr Doug Hall was the director at the Queensland Art Gallery at the time. The Asian department was led by Ms Suhanya Raffel. The team worked hard and cooperated really well; they were very efficient, careful and accurate. They communicated with me throughout the whole process.

ZU: Another work I enjoyed a lot was the portrait you created for the paediatrician Dr John Yu. I remember you told me that that came about through Mr Simon Elliott's recommendation. Each time I visit the National Portrait Gallery, I see it.

> *Dr John Yu was Australian of the Year in 1996 for his achievements in medicine and education, especially children's health. He was also the Chancellor of the University of New South Wales from 2000 to 2006.*

AX: Dr John Yu was a successful role model for Australian people especially for Chinese people here in Australia. That was why he was awarded as the Australian of the year in 1996. In 2002, the National Portrait Gallery approached me and asked if I would do his portrait. I didn't know him personally before that. The Portrait Gallery had looked for an artist to portray him for a few years. It is the gallery's practice to commission one portrait or a few per year for their collection. So that year, they asked me. They said they had watched me for a couple of years and knew my work was good. It took a while before the gallery sought out the fund. I was told then it was their most expensive commission up to the time. [laughs] Anyway, it is the only commission I've done so far. It took me two years to complete the portrait. As for the ideas of that particular work, I was thinking about how to represent John Yu's Chinese background and his contribution to this country.

ZU: That representation came through very clearly. I saw photos of you working on his mould in his backyard.

AX: I only made one set of moulds of him. [My wife] Ma Li helped me.

ZU: In 2001, you won the National Sculpture Prize at the National Gallery of Australia, but they were not porcelain sculptures. Why did you choose a new material, cloisonné?

AX: I thought I shouldn't repeat myself. I wanted to change the record and widen the scope of my work. Once I started to look, I realised there was a lot I could do. At the end of 1999 and the beginning of 2000, I visited cloisonné and lacquer manufacturers on the outskirts of Beijing. The Beijing

Carved Lacquer Factory was government run at the time. I made five bust works and three full-length figures. Soon after, the factory closed down. Since then I haven't been able to make lacquer work.

ZU: Let's talk at a deeper level that goes beyond your work. You made the comment that the motifs on your sculptures – lotus flowers, birds, water patterns and landscape that you borrowed from traditional Chinese art – were the result of being away from China.

AX: As we say, 'you don't really see the whole of Mt Lu because you're on it'. When I was in China, I didn't notice much about these patterns. In those days, artists' practice was more towards the Western modern and contemporary art rather than traditional Chinese art. After I left China, I was missing my motherland and the feeling of intimacy with the familiar, so it became possible for me to gradually develop this interest. Perhaps I recognised it more clearly when I had enough distance from it in both physical and psychological senses. It confirmed my standpoint. By contrast, while I was in China, I only thought about making experimental, contemporary art. But so-called modern art was actually much separate from the Chinese tradition. Traditional Chinese art has continued for thousands of years right up to the present. There must be a reason it happened like this. It's the same for Western art. There have been thousands and thousands of artworks over the years, but only those created by the masters have endured. The reason they have been recorded in art history is because the work is really good.

Looking at it from another angle – we've got our own uniqueness with our own cultural background and quality...

It's the same principle I suppose for artists who come from Western backgrounds and traditions. We all naturally learn from our ancestors, from what we are familiar with and live with, and we create and contribute our best, depending on who we are and what we are good at … Of course, we also learn from each other …

ZU: Ah, that gives me an insight into your ideas. I wonder what do you think was the main reason that the sculptures were so much appreciated by Australians – so much so that you won the National Sculpture Prize?

AX: I think it is the creativity in combining the two halves [Western and Chinese art] that makes it stand out. Without this fusion, if it had just been a matter of the craftsmanship of cloisonné or a bare figurative form, it would have been ordinary and decorative only. I always liked Western realistic figurative sculptures. Chinese art does have realistic sculptures, but they are not realistic like in Western art. Qin terracotta warriors, Buddhist statutes and tomb figures are good examples. They contain realistic components such as facial expressions, body structure and shape but they are idealised and often symbolic. The way the figure is refined must have something to do with Chinese philosophy.

ZU: Aren't your works also idealised? One of the purposes of this book is to document how Chinese art has influenced Australian perceptions about China, Chinese culture and people, and how contemporary artists have renewed people's perceptions while retaining the essence of Chinese tradition. Your work exemplifies this.

AX: I could only make this work because I had left China, I'm afraid. I questioned what was the pinnacle of Chinese tradition and how to utilise it. It's not that we should throw away tradition; it's a matter of how to ingest it, and then apply it.

ZU: Let's talk about your creations from the perspectives of subject, materials, size and working environment. Have all of these changed?

AX: Until recent years, I've worked in many different materials and techniques. One thing that has remained is the realistic life-size human form. I've been considering what to do next, seeking a change, as always. In the past, the essential thing remained the same despite all the cosmetic changes. I am satisfied with each work, but I have not gone very far beyond myself. I strive for the best but the best doesn't necessary mean perfect in technique and craftsmanship only. I mean when it's exactly at the just-right point in an artistic sense.

ZU: The concept of 'just-right' depends on an artist's own unique sensibility.

AX: Yes. I always aim for a very high point. For example, a stone may be rough, but when it is put together with a body cast in bronze [his 'Evolutionaura' series], making it right and finishing it a certain way is what I mean by the 'just-right point'.

ZU: Indeed. Your 'Concrete Forest' (2009) could be a very good example.

AX: Yes. The material sounds rough but it's artistically expressive and can be worked in very fine detail. I wanted to move away from craftsmanship at that time. Concrete is a material usually used for building construction, as we know. It's cheap, heavy, rough and, not generally an art material but it can achieve some very high artistic effects if used well.

ZU: There's a particular topic that I have always wanted to discuss with you, and that is beauty. It is in your work. It makes your work enduring and it has a very strong impact on viewers. Where does it come from?

AX: Beauty is profound. It is very powerful and also very subtle. Perhaps I cannot explain it clearly.

Many contemporary art works stand out because they are surprising, shocking and confrontational. It has to be new, it must be creative. Newness stimulates viewers and touches them. But the new can also be inappropriate, evil and extreme. There are artists who kill animals, and use human blood, parts of human corpses or even whole ones. One artist even canned his own faeces, then sealed and labelled them as artworks. Works may be new and creative because something hasn't been done before. They can be stimulating, shocking or irritating but it's not beauty. It is not necessarily nor automatically a positive or inspirational creation. Beauty is important and essential to me. It is a subtle accumulation over time. I don't think I have any secrets. I don't follow any formula. Apart from separating the dross from true art, culture and traditions, the rest is more relying on one's instinct and sensibility, I suppose. One point I need to stress is that beauty is only one element of art but it has never been the only one.

ZU: Your work embodies an unusual beauty. All the figures you've created are in a state of stillness. It resonates with Chinese Taoist thinking: *wuwei* or non-action.

When viewers look at the work, it encompasses movement, contemplation and dialogue with the work. Is this your intention?

AX: I believe I am a perfectionist. Stillness is a natural expression for me. When I come up with ideas, I usually don't incorporate elements that are noisy, messy, filthy, rotten or raw. Other artists put objects straight into their works, or pour paint randomly and leave it there. Perhaps it's pretty much an expression of my personality as I'm quite quiet, introverted, shy and slow ...

ZU: You deal with rough materials, such as concrete, but the finish is very beautiful.

AX: I wouldn't disagree, but like I said – only if you handle it precisely. That's where art is created. My concrete works deal with rough materials, but there are some fine details for viewers to see. For example, there are holes formed by the stalks of leaves and the fine texture of the leaves' veins curves along human outlines that viewers can appreciate slowly.

ZU: Seeing your work makes me feel that you make your art with sincerity. It is not religious, but it is a belief.

AX: Thank you for saying this. Indeed, that should be the way. I always have a sensation of modesty and extreme deference when I face art and create art. It's a bit like a pious Buddhist who crawls on all fours, praying, when on a pilgrimage. Art is something that is seen from above, like spiritual gods. I'm not religious but I guess art is a form of religious experience, although I know many artists claim that art is just something for fun.

ZU: I'm always interested in transcendence, searching for what cannot be realised or fulfilled by reality.

AX: Yes. It comforts the mind. Or by contrast, it is a way of releasing tension; it heals.

Everything in your life, including knowledge and experience – all those things that cannot be expressed or entrusted – is given to art. From this perspective, art is indispensable to one's spiritual world.

ZU: It seems the beauty we are discussing is a kind of sublime, lasting beauty.

AX: Yes. I hope so. When I make art, I never consider the market for the work. But it is interesting that my works have happened to be quite popular.

ZU: Do you mean that you want your work to appeal to all, both refined and popular tastes? To be admired and enjoyed by those more and less cultured?

AX: Hmmm ... you could say that. There's the possibility of multi-layered reading ... My intention is nothing more than to make art which I am faithful to and sincere about.

ZU: What is your definition of art?

AX: My definition … [laughs and avoids a direct answer] Ha ha, I did have a definition of art a long time ago. Perhaps it can be put in this way: Art is 'useless things' made faithfully and sincerely by 'useless people'. It's magic that can touch people's minds and souls. However, if we put aside explanations of art and talk about its function and structure, then first it must have an idea (concept). Secondly, it must be new (creative). Third, there must be a precise way of dealing with the materials (including idea/concepts as materials). The combination of the three makes for good art.

For example, if a painter paints a portrait of someone, it doesn't necessarily mean it's art. Painting is related to a major part of art, but it's not automatically art. To be able to paint is just a skill. It's as same as being a blacksmith, a carpenter or a potter. There is of cause, a certain level of artistic creativity involved among all these activities but depends on how much … What's also necessary is for one's mind, the reflection of one's soul, one's contemplation and creation to be embedded into the work. Otherwise, it's only a functional craft including for decoration. And if you don't have original ideas, then there's no art.

ZU: I agree.

I've noticed in articles I've read that you have particular views about traditional and contemporary China, and about the relationship between the Western world and China. How do you resolve the contradictions between these different values and ethics?

AX: I've found that Chinese culture is often used as a label on an object. Artists intentionally put it on their work for branding.

ZU: You may not put such labels on yourself, but you cannot disagree with them because you have referenced Chinese traditional patterns and motifs, and used Chinese traditional craftsmanship. People have labelled you because of this.

AX: I know. But I think there are big differences in the way Chinese heritage can be incorporated. The method I adopt is to digest and grasp it thoroughly, mastering it through a comprehensive study of the culture. I only absorb its brilliance and excellence to nurture my art. It is like nurturing a plant instead of just taking the fruit and labelling it as Chinese. From this angle, some so-called Chinese art is actually superficial. The way I create really comes from the heart. As I develop a concept, I try to think over all the possibilities. To look at it from another angle: Chinese-ness perhaps part of our nature. It's just there, existing; there's no need to make a thing of it. All artists from all over the world contribute their art, each from their own position, perspective and coming from their own heritage and culture. There is no need to claim what we are; we are just being ourselves.

ZU: How do you work with the craftsmen in the manufacture of your sculptures? Do you explain to them which pattern to paint?

AX: The patterns already exist. They are painted on plates or vases. I like the patterns they use. Most of the lacquer and cloisonné works use the same crafting process. I visit many workshops to find different styles to make the works. Then I choose the ones I think are good. By that, I mean that the style is more refined and elegant. Not too popular, common or lowbrow. Then I talk to the craftsmen.

Through talking, I can judge their capacity to adapt and understand, and see how they respond to others. If we get along and I think they are good, then I go and see their boss. That's the money side of the process.

ZU: Do you make the busts yourself?

AX: Yes. Partially. I mainly work in some of the initial procedures such as researching the mouldings, refining each very first original positive cast, overall supervision and other work wherever and whenever I need to ...

ZU: Does it ever go wrong when you take it to the factory?

AX: Yes. For example, once the craftsman painted a necklace on my bust piece. He thought it was a great idea. [laughs] There have been other problems too such as cracks or a fall in the kiln.

The craftsmen had difficulties painting my sculptures at the beginning. They were used to painting vases and platters that are always symmetrical, round-shaped, more or less 2D images. My works aren't like that.

ZU: You have been working with craftsmen for many years. Have they increased their prices?

AX: Of course. For example, if they made one piece for 500 yuan some 20 years ago, they would ask for over 10,000 yuan, even more than 100,000 yuan nowadays. Before I could afford them more easily; now it is increasingly more difficult.

ZU: Goodness me!

AX: It's inflation, caused by increased living costs and people's increased greed I guess. Taking in the larger picture, in the run-up to the Olympics in 2008 and under the pressure of the global economic recession, the Chinese government released a 4 trillion RMB yuan stimulus package [US$586 billion]. The whole nation was digesting this money. All the small enterprises increased their charges.

ZU: Has the quality remained the same?

AX: Yes, but you need to supervise and keep an eye on them, otherwise they can play tricks on you. For example, they add tung oil (paulownia) or kerosene into the latex gel, to dilute it so as to make more profit. It looks the same but the mould made of the diluted latex gel is thinner and softer, not good enough to hold its shape, and it lasts a much shorter time. There are many tricks you have to be careful with ... working in China is not plain sailing.

ZU: Oh dear!

When artists are recorded in history it is often because their work reflects that time or an event. You have been recognised as an iconic model because you combine Chinese traditional art with Western art. You have made great contributions to enhancing Chinese culture. How do you see your work fitting in?

AX: I know it's what people say to encourage me. Thanks very much. But I actually do not see myself as that important, nor do I see myself as in the middle like a bridge. I am just an ordinary individual. I am free to float in between. When I moved to live in Australia, I more or less lost my roots in

China I'm afraid. I have personal reservations about today's China. I cannot agree with it. There are many restrictions on free speech. It's still under one party, a one-man dictatorship without genuine freedom or democracy. Here in Australia – where I call home now, because of my lack of English ability – I haven't had a true experience of reading English literature. When I watch a movie or the daily TV news, I don't understand it 100 per cent. There are communication barriers, language barriers. Although I've been learning all these years, it's far from good enough. Even in a conversation with a friend I can't express myself 100 per cent. It doesn't go deep enough.

ZU: Floating is a very good position. Perhaps there are things that are too meaningful to speak about.

AX: Yes and no. Things are lost in translation. [laughs] But I rather like this kind of displacement or loss. It is a bit like poetry. There is a distance and a space between the words. Although it looks like a broken sentence, the gap in between is perfect for one to imagine. You can fill it up with anything you fancy. That's the place where you can manipulate, mess about, work on things ... So, for me, dislocation and being caught in between Australia and China, although it seems I am at a disadvantage with nothing to rely on or lean on, I consider it to be a good vantage point.

ZU: I also see in it a reflection of one characteristic of a Chinese intellectual, that of being a hermit. Your busts praise nature. You demonstrate sensitivity towards the human condition. The patterns you use – bamboo, lotus flowers and grape veins – are symbolic and self-contained.

AX: Indeed! But in the past, intellectuals chose to hide, to live in solitude. In contemporary life, I choose to drift.

ZU: You have made the most of it by enjoying your free state.

Ah Xian would have not looked around to discover, but readers will see that he is not drifting alone. According to the law of nature, everything is interconnected and in constant change. It resonates with the Tao. A central thread of sincerity and hope holds firm.

Chapter III

Watch the turmoil of beings,
but contemplate their return.
Each separate being in the universe
returns to the common source.
Returning to the source is serenity.

Lao-tzu, *Tao Te Ching*, Chapter 16

The Value of Adversity

This chapter's title, The Value of Adversity, is taken from my *I Ching* throws. It shows how to overcome difficulties through reflection.

The chapter contains four conversations with Chinese-Australian artists – Xiao Lu, Wang Zhiyuan, Lin Chunyan and Shen Shaomin. Their situation is part of a phenomenon whereby a large number of Chinese went overseas in the 1990s and returned to China around 2000. It represents one of the main reasons for writing this book.

My questions were to discern the reasons for their return, to find out what made them decide to leave Australia and to follow up their creative work since they left Australia.

One thing these artists have in common was the desire to make art that transcends geographical boundaries. Regardless of their environment, whether political or natural, their creative environment had its own measure, value and sensibility that was deeply rooted in China. As the old Chinese saying goes – 'A child never thinks its mother is ugly, and a dog never shuns its owner's home, however shabby' – meaning don't forget where you come from. China provided Xiao, Wang, Lin and Shen with the possibility of continuing to make art, or simply to make a living. To use their words, life and art are one. However, every one of them acknowledged the influence of their Australian experience and the important role it played in their life and art.

Xiao, Wang, Lin and Shen, unlike Guan Wei and Ah Xian, are not known to Australians. Some people may know their works, but few appreciate their contribution to Australian art. To recognise the equal importance of both sides of the story,

I consulted the *I Ching* to uncover the hidden implications. I asked: If I were on the threshold between Australia and China, in a situation of choosing to stay or leave, what would be the main factor to help me to make the decision? I found an answer in hexagram 39, *Jian*, Adversity.

ABOVE: THE ABYSS, WATER
BELOW: KEEPING STILL, MOUNTAIN

It predicates adversity which appears over the course of time and which can be overcome. Then it gives instructions as to how to overcome it. The advice in the judgment is 'Perseverance brings good fortune.' The depiction is:

THE IMAGE
Water on the mountain;
The image of obstruction.
Thus the superior man turns his attention to himself
And moulds his character.

Difficulties and obstructions throw a man back upon himself. While the inferior man seeks to put the blame on other persons, bewailing his fate, the superior man seeks the error within himself, and through this introspection the external obstacle becomes for him an occasion for inner enrichment and education.

When Xiao, Wang, Lin and Shen confronted difficulties they experienced in Australia that couldn't be overcome directly, they returned to China. The situation ahead of them was unclear, however, they obtained great success. Why was that? First, as the Tao had predicted, 'it is wise to pause in view of danger and retreat'. Their actions resonated with the

I Ching's direction, 'one must join forces with friends of like mind'. Secondly, their retreat manifested the great wisdom of knowing when to turn back, without bias, aggression or halting. I have come to realise that 'unswerving inner purpose brings good fortune in the end. An obstruction that lasts only for a time is useful for self-development. This is the value of adversity.'

'I came back!'

Conversation with Xiao Lu
30 May 2017

Xiao Lu (b. 1962) is the first female performance artist in China. Her parents are artists and professors who taught at the National Academy of Fine Arts (formerly Zhejiang Academy of Fine Arts). Xiao Lu's performance art encompasses emotions that are sensual and radical.

Xiao had a solid classical art education from the age of 17. She studied oil painting at Zhejiang Academy of Fine Arts between 1984 and 1988. In Feburary1989, she transformed her graduation work into an installation/performance piece called 'Dialogue' and exhibited in the 'China Avant-Garde' exhibition at the National Art Museum, Beijing. At the opening of the exhibition, Xiao Lu fired two gunshots at her installation. Because of her action, the Chinese government shut down the exhibition that same day. Four months later, the June Fourth Incident took place, leading to a period of cultural repression. There were no public exhibitions allowed. Many artists moved overseas, to North America, Europe and Australia. Xiao Lu went to Sydney.

She participated in the 'Twelve Contemporary Chinese Artists' exhibition at the University of Sydney in 1991, organised by Mabel Lee and curated by Archibald McKenzie. In 1992 she participated in the 'Orientations – The Emperor's New Clothes' group exhibition at Irving Galleries. Xiao returned to Beijing in 1997. She has shown regularly since 2003 in China and internationally.

Xiao Lu and I have known each other since 1979. We both studied and boarded at the Fine Arts School Affiliated to the Chinese Central Academy of Fine Arts (Fuzhong) for four years.

I had this conversation with Xiao Lu at the library of the Museum of Contemporary Art on 30 May 2017. She talked about her signature piece, her performance work, 'Dialogue'.

ZU: Let's start from Fuzhong days, when we were studying together. Do you think that period influenced your art?

XIAO: Of course! The impact was ... ah ... [exhaling heavily] enormous and deep.

You know those times in the girls' dormitory at Fuzhong, when the lights were off, we would talk about the relations between men and women. We really didn't have a clue, it was just fantasies. But, in a sense, we were physically and mentally mature. Therefore, even though I hadn't been told a thing, inside I was ready.

So ... [exhaling again] I might often have sublimated my emotions. And that sublimation, that displacement, perhaps was what forced me to take the path of contemporary art.

ZU: What was your intention when you created 'Dialogue'?

XIAO: I have repeated myself so many times about this. [forces a smile] Perhaps, when I was young, I was too much entangled with emotions. If you look at my work over the years, emotion has always been a focal point. [exhaling again] So ... when I made this work in 1988, you could see from the installation that the dialogue was between a man and a woman. But the telephone handset in the middle is swinging down. This means that there is an obstacle to the dialogue

– it is impossible to communicate. To me the installation and the performance is one work. It expresses the confused emotions between men and women.

ZU: You've often said, and in fact you just said it again, that when you made the 'Dialogue' installation, what you did was not related to the political environment in China at the time. Your work was all about humanity and freedom but it was indirect. So, in that sense, your story seems to merge with social phenomena. Can you say how that makes you feel?

XIAO: In 1989, this work occurred in a special historical context. This gave it a new interpretation.

I have experienced so many things. I believe as an artist, the work I create and how the public perceives it are two things – two parts.

As an artist, I have inspiration – many inspirations. It's just like a baby that comes into the world. Society sees whatever they want to see in it. Various possibilities exist. However, I was the one carrying it, so I know more clearly how it came about.

When we read a novel, for example, the writer might have had something very personal to say when writing the book. As a reader, we are moved by a certain narrative. That's because we relate that story to our own experiences. But that's got nothing to do with the author's experience. So when the work came out in 1989, the circumstances surrounding it were indivisible from historical events. At the same time, the work also carries a lot of meaning.

Because of all this, I don't feel particularly bothered. An artist neither knows the future once the work's been created nor has any control over how people perceive the work. So as long as the work's title and date are correct, I don't mind what people write about it. Viewing the work is a recreation. Contemporary art leaves space for viewers to interpret.

ZU: What is the link between your first performance and the work you do now?

XIAO: I am very clear when I make a work. I have to make sure the work will touch me. Only then can I complete it.

ZU: How about the environment?

XIAO: Whatever the art trends are around me, they are not really related to me directly. I am interested in and look for points where I relate to society or a particular state within myself.

ZU: How about the outcomes? It seems accidents often happen during your performances.

XIAO: For years I have worked on performance art., it always makes me excited if an accident happens because it is something outside my expectation. Accidents are a necessity in my performance art. The way I perform is different from a stage performance. I don't normally rehearse, That includes when there is a sudden change during the performance that wasn't part of my design. I have no plan for what to do but I make up my mind on the spot. I accept any consequences that are a result of the sudden change. That's why my work can exist regardless.

ZU: It requires spontaneity!

XIAO: Performance occurs in the instant. No other art form does this.

ZU: Hmmm ... Actually I think accidents, or chance, happen in all good art. Perhaps performance is the art form that suits you best.

XIAO: I also think my personality makes it possible. If someone else was doing it, maybe there would be no performance. For example, if someone told you that you can't do something, most likely you wouldn't do it. Right?

ZU: Can you give me an example?

XIAO: That day in Venice (2013), my plan was to wear the mud I had carried from China, and then to wash it off with Venetian water. It was a conceptual work, seemingly making a connection between China's Grand Canal and Venice. At the beginning, they agreed that I could do it in the river outside the gallery. On the opening day, they suddenly changed their mind and told me I couldn't perform it.

ZU: Oh. Did they give a reason?

XIAO: It was because the museum was Catholic. Nudity was not allowed.

ZU: Oh!

XIAO: The day before the opening, they cancelled my performance. They took away the mud I brought from China too. I was thinking about what to do ... After the opening speech, I took off my clothes, ran outside and jumped into the river ... I didn't tell anyone. I had been thinking about it. The inspiration was stimulated by the site. I can respond quickly if the situation changes suddenly.

Art is an attitude – an attitude towards a happening. Performance art is the quickest response compared with other art forms. It suits my style.

ZU: Are there many performing artists like you? It must be a challenge for curators and exhibition organisers.

XIAO: Some galleries do not like to exhibit performance art because artists cannot be managed. There are a lot of spontaneous reactions. You can't plan beforehand.

I now have a very good curator. We have worked together very well in the past two years ... He doesn't interfere, whatever I do! [laughs]

ZU: How do you work with curators?

XIAO: I have sketches. I show the curator my draft. But often I change the plan. For example, materials bought for installation works sometimes are different from what I wanted. I may need to make adjustments because of the materials.

ZU: I can understand that. The differences between one material and another sometimes are small yet important.

XIAO: Because of that, I don't use assistants. I deal with manufacturers directly.

ZU: I like that!

XIAO: Many artists use assistants – factory line production, I can't do that. I need to see every detail, and feel it. The subtlety cannot be explained. The assistants didn't know how artists feel so they could make the work completely different from the artist's idea. My record in changing my performance plan was under one hour. They gave me the wrong material. I couldn't relate to it.

I have a routine – if the performance takes place indoors, I must see the space. I am interested in architecture, I am very sensitive to my surroundings. I create the work based on the space. It's like giving birth at that place.

For outdoor performances I respond to the environment. In Chinese, we say 'Immediate objects provoke thoughts and feelings'.

ZU: It must be nerve-racking for museum curators.

XIAO: Yes. My experience working with museums is that once the planning has been done, you cannot change the performance. But I always change it. [smiles] So, I prefer it when museums exhibit my completed works.

ZU: Is it easier if the curators know your work? That way they might be more relaxed and trust you to make the work.

XIAO: That's right. Actually, for mature performance artists, it is important to have that trust because they will be responsible for themselves. The more trust you place on them, the more responsibility they will take.

ZU: Absolutely.

XIAO: And the reverse is true – the more you interfere, the less creative they will be. You know what I mean. It's impossible for me to be constrained.

ZU: Talking about being restrained, what happened during the time you spent in Sydney? And when did you go back to China?

XIAO: I came to Sydney at the end of 1989 and returned to Beijing in 1997.

ZU: What is your memory of that time?

XIAO: Now, looking back and examining myself, I think I had serious psychological problems. After the traumatic experience at Fuzhong, I had been very depressed. 'Dialogue' in the 1989 national exhibition, perhaps, was me breaking out after a long period of suppression. But what happened was that after the explosion, I couldn't confront the work myself.

ZU: Hmmm ...

XIAO: You see, I am not a conceptual artist. I make work based on my own experiences and emotions. A complicated sexual relationship could lead to the creation of a work. It is totally different from some male artists. They have sets of theories to boast about. I have different ways of thinking.

Moreover, in the 80s, you had to know how to talk about your work. You know, at Zhemei (National Art Academy) everyone was talking about conceptual art. I felt like fainting when I heard their endless talk.

ZU: The sad thing was what they talked about was merely words and the words were not reflected in the work.

XIAO: [shakes her head] But I made the work. It's out there, right?

It was totally out of my expectation that the work would have such a huge impact. Who knew what kind of shit luck it was that the work would astonish the world! I knew, and I always knew quite clearly what the work was about and why I created the work. But what I didn't know was the outcome.

After the 89 exhibition, I couldn't make work for a long time. Why was that? I have been thinking about this …

ZU: Why was it?

XIAO: Because I didn't have the confidence.

> *Xiao Lu revealed that one of the main reasons she lacked confidence because she was silenced. People (no names mentioned) were talking about her work as her voice. She admitted that it had been a compromise when she collaborated with her partner at the time.*

Today I am very confident. Since 2003, I have made many new works, and revised over 50 works. At present, I am making work independently, one after another. This kind of confidence is very real! Let me tell you, you must make work! You must work alone!

ZU: Yes.

XIAO: After a certain period, people know what your work is about. You will be strong enough to confront anything. I felt deeply in 89 that my name was bigger than my ability. I thought I'd been lucky because I had a big platform. But the work was too successful for me to cope with. I had my own psychological problems, I was manipulated.

If 'Dialogue' hadn't been so famous, if I had married and had children, I would have become a housewife for the rest of my life.

ZU: Do you think so?

XIAO: True.

ZU: No. You are who you are and you always will be that person.

XIAO: Perhaps I wasn't in a real environment. Truth is very important to me. Without truth I cannot make work.

ZU: I am glad you succeeded! [smiles]

XIAO: The '15 shots' work in 2003 was a product of releasing anger.

On 19 October 2003, Xiao Lu performed 'Fifteen Shots … From 1989 to 2003', firing 15 bullets at her self-portraits in Beijing. She stated: 'I am no good at theoretical explanations, and even worse at talking about art. All I know is real life. Work, for me, is an inner necessity. It can be a painting or a poem. Perhaps it requires a gun. All of this is decided by your own psychological tendencies, your disposition. This is nothing that can be explained by the word "art", but it's rather a survival instinct, your very life.'

I came back! Xiao Lu's energy has returned to me! [laughs]

ZU: You liberated yourself!

XIAO: Yes. Someone who has been to hell will become fearless. The point is I can accept any consequence I have created. My personality decides my fate.

After that I made 'Sperm', 'Wedlock' – many works! I came to realise the reason I can make art again, the return of me, is because I now can confront myself. My real self is the source of my works.

ZU: I remember you told me that 'Sperm' (2006) is in the White Rabbit Gallery's collection.

XIAO: Yes. Wang Zhiyuan really liked 'Sperm' so he recommended it to Judith [Neilson]. People had different opinions about that work.

ZU: I am so glad that Wang Zhiyuan did that. I remember seeing the installation at our Fuzhong group exhibition at Permanence Gallery. It was controversial because you touched upon a taboo topic in China. Many people didn't understand it. It's great that White Rabbit Gallery gave it a home.

XIAO: Judith saw the work at the Long March Space and collected the whole set of work including the video. It was my only installation work for this piece.

ZU: White Rabbit Gallery provides a window for Australians to see China. They have around a thousand visitors a day.

XIAO: Indeed. It is an excellent window. When all is said and done around the world about China, the understanding has been rather one sided. But Judith wanted to know China, so she went to China. That is very rare. I think it is wonderful that there is an organisation that pays close attention to contemporary Chinese art.

ZU: Absolutely.

How about Geoff Raby? He was the Ambassador to China in 2010. He collected one of your shooting prints too, didn't he?

XIAO: Yes. He collected the 'Open Fire' (2005). Geoff hosted my book launch at the Australian Embassy in Beijing.

In 2010 Xiao Lu's novel based on her personal story 'Dialogue' was published by Hong Kong University Press.

ZU: That's right. You see what I am getting at? [smiles] It's time for you to come back to Sydney.

XIAO: Alas! My whole life has been entangled with love! So, if I have love, I will come back to Sydney. [laughs]

Our conversation concluded in a silly childlike way, just like when we were in our teens at the Fuzhong.

'Our art is our world and our world is our experience'

Conversation with Wang Zhiyuan
20 JULY 2017

Wang Zhiyuan was born in Tianjin in 1958. He migrated to Sydney, Australia in 1989 and returned to China to live and work in 2002. Wang Zhiyuan is a Chinese-Australian contemporary artist known for his giant underpants installation, 'Object of Desire' (2008), and 'Thrown to the Wind' (2010), a 36-foot-high sculpture made entirely from discarded plastic containers. His works are in the National Gallery of Australia, Queensland Art Gallery and Gallery of Modern Art and the White Rabbit Gallery collections.

I first met Wang Zhiyuan in 1983 when we studied at Central Academy of Fine Arts (CAFA) in Beijing. On 20 July 2017, we decided to do our one-hour conversation for the book. We met at Well Co Café on Glebe Point Road, Glebe. Well Co was a small internet café, a hang-out spot for old friends back in the early 90s. It serves good coffee against a background of red brick walls with posters from the 90s. When we walked upstairs, the wooden steps made creaking noises. Upstairs, it was not busy, although the music was a bit distracting.

This conversation is about contemporary art and cultural barriers, about the China-Australia art school and society.

ZU: Among all the artists I have talked to for this book, your background is unique. You had extensive formal art training in both China and Australia. If you compare these two different systems, what are your thoughts about the impact of art education on art?

WANG: When I was in China, you and I were much the same in that we were under the CAFA system. I stayed within it for ten years – first as a student for four years, then I taught at Fuzhong for five years. I lived at CAFA, so I was always inside the system. I knew the teachers, the students. I knew the whole system inside out. After ten years inside the system in China, I came to Australia and stayed for ten years. There I was outside the system. I was completely on my own – freelancing. I experienced both sides.

ZU: Was it difficult to adapt at the beginning?

WANG: Of course!

Wang Zhiyuan commented that he thought art education in 80s China had been narrow and limited because they only had access to pre-production prints of the old masters and 19th century Russian realists. Not even CAFA, the best art institution in China, had any post-modernist art resources.

It is useful to have training in realism. We learnt a skill. But in my experience, when I first came to Sydney, it was very hard to adjust. I was unfamiliar with Australian contemporary art. I was struggling to find a way to use my skills and to get involved in that society, to express my feelings, especially in the face of the two cultures and the language barriers.

ZU: I understand what you are saying. I had a very similar experience. What I found frustrating was that there wasn't much I could do at the time.

WANG: Of course, it requires a few years to get used to it.

ZU: Sometimes hardship stimulates creativity, doesn't it? I like your 'Two from One' series that you made in 1997. Did you show them anywhere?

WANG: In 1997, I was in the 'In & Out' exhibition curated by Huangpu Binghui.

'In & Out – Contemporary Chinese Art from China and Australia' was an international touring exhibition from 1997 to 2000, organised by Beijing-born curator and critic Huangpu Binghui. The artists were Ah Xian, Xiao Xian, Guan Wei and Wang Zhiyuan from Sydney and six other Beijing-based artists.

It was a touring exhibition that started in Singapore, then it came to Australia. It was first shown at SCA (Sydney College of the Arts) – the first Chinese art show they had ever hosted. They made three exhibition halls available to us. I showed my ten-piece relief sculpture, the 'Fragments: Two from One' series. The director Richard Dunn personally curated the SCA show. My work was hung in the main gallery in the centre of the front wall.

ZU: Aha! Was that how you connected with SCA and undertook your master's degree study?

WANG: I started at SCA in January 1999. That was just by chance. It was not my own initiative.

Wang explained that towards to the closing of the exhibition, Richard Dunn invited him to apply for studying at SCA for a master's degree course. Wang's application was accepted in 1998.

To be able to complete my master's degree in SCA, I should thank Richard Dunn, who was also my supervisor.

I worked very hard, participated in SCA's activities, such as seminars and lectures. I did a lot of reading. But generally speaking I was confused. I could only understand some words or get half the meaning. But I learned a lot.

ZU: I see. You made great progress within two years.

WANG: [recalling his memories excitedly] Writing my thesis took me four months. Making the works took me three months. There were 72 graduates in my year. My work was hung in the main gallery in the centre of the front wall again. My thesis was excellent. I still use it today!

ZU: It must be a really good thesis.

WANG: I don't know if it's good but it played very important role in my career. It provided a clear path for my artistic development. It enabled me continue to build on it, expanding from it.

ZU: You went to CAFA and SCA. What were the differences between them?

WANG: Hmmm. I think the main difference was not the content, but the structure. I remember when I was at CAFA between 80 and 84, it was like military training. We lived on campus. We had to get up early in the morning. Our PE teacher led us on a long run. On orientation day, the dean of administration summoned us and said, 'There are 34 students in your year. The ratio is 3:1. That means every student has three staff.' That included the boiler workers [adds Wang sarcastically]. 'You must appreciate your good fortune! Therefore no dating is allowed. Everyone must behave properly!'

ZU: Now, looking back, how stupid was that! I can't believe that at the time we thought it was normal.

WANG: CAFA provided accommodation for us. It was like a military camp, don't you think? You thought you were protected, that you were being taken care of. We were made to feel that we had responsibilities, and also that we were valued.

ZU: I never thought about it like that. But I do know that every one of us, even today, has a sense of superiority because we went to CAFA. And I did enjoy visiting any art museum for free!

WANG: Because CAFA was so hard to get in to, when we came out, we felt like we had a golden ring shining above our head, engraved with names like Rembrandt, Picasso or Matisse.

In Australia it was totally different. Regardless of whether you were an undergraduate or a postgraduate, the school didn't interfere in your life. Students lived off campus. Because of that, the barriers between the institution and society were very low, almost invisible. By contrast, CAFA built its wall extremely high. After I became a freelancer mixing in with society, I felt very strongly that it's a hundred times better without the fence than with it.

ZU: I think your observation of the differences is quite correct. But I still believe that to build a strong foundation at the early stage of art learning is crucial. Why do you think the Western approach is better?

WANG: Because in the long term what we do means that we will never have a job. Art expresses the self. No company employs you to express yourself. The disadvantage of that high fence is that when you emerge from inside it, suddenly you realise you don't have a nanny any more. You are left alone. No one cares about you.

ZU: Didn't you teach at Fuzhong after you graduated from CAFA?

WANG: Yes I did! But because I changed from having a nanny to becoming a nanny doesn't disprove my point. I was still on the inside. What I mean is most artists have to go into the real world.

From this perspective, I really appreciate the freer Western approach. It inspires students and encourages them to develop the skills to explore independently. Because it gives you this sort of experience from the beginning, you develop contacts beyond the academy. You have the teacher–student connections and the resources, but you also engage with society, while experiencing the life of a real artist. You get to know what your working conditions will be like in future.

Society, by which I mean commodity society, has no capacity to support artists, except in Western countries like Australia where the government provides funding. There's a small number of grant recipients but you only get a little bit of money and it's by sheer luck. You can only live on it for six months or a year. Privately donated money also allows certain artists a subsistence living.

[Neither system is perfect but] I believe Western art education is the best environment for artists.

ZU: It is a realistic approach.

WANG: Yes. The art institution is an academy, but at the same time, it's also a community. It's different in China, where art institutions are ivory towers.

ZU: It sounds like in 1999 you were having an interesting time exploring life in Sydney.

WANG: Actually, 1999 was my hardest year in Sydney. I was alone. I lived in a flat in front of Bronwyn Thomas's house in Camperdown. That was also the year I undertook my master's study at SCA.

ZU: Tell me about Bronwyn Thomas.

WANG: Bronwyn was a very nice lady who had close friendships with Chinese people. I lived there for more than six months. Half the room was used as storage, and there was a double bed in the other half. Living conditions were basic. I cooked in her house. The flat had a very interesting history. Many Chinese artists had lived there, including Guan Wei and Liu Ping. When Claire and Nick came back from China, they also lived there. When I first arrived in Sydney, I used to go there sometimes for get-togethers and dinners.

Bronwyn went to Beijing in the late 80s. She made friends with Brian Wallace. She often asked me to go to exhibition openings with her. Without her enthusiastic support I might have been really depressed.

Bronwyn Thomas (1923–2000) was born in Melbourne. She was the director of the Bonython Gallery in 1971–74 and director of the Australian Centre for Photography in 1974–78. In her later life, she became interested in Chinese art and culture. She first visited China in 1980 and subsequently studied Chinese at the University of Sydney and in Beijing. She lived in Beijing in 1989–92, teaching English and assisting galleries with exhibitions. On her return to Sydney, she continued to promote Chinese artists, especially those who had settled in Australia.

ZU: That's what we call it: experiencing joy in misery.

WANG: That's right.

ZU: I see your point. But at the same time, I think you are contradicting yourself. You seem to be a great supporter of the way of life for artists in Australia, so why did you return to China?

WANG: After 11 years living in Sydney, I just really missed Beijing – deeply, in my bones. I missed it every day!

Australia is great for Australians with no language problems, but I don't have a talent for language. The problem I had living in Sydney was the language. I got no pleasure from it no matter how hard I tried. To live a basic life, just eating and sleeping, is not a problem as long as I have work to do, but to live happily means using language, including reading. I couldn't enjoy the pleasure of reading in English.

ZU: I believe you started showing in 1999 at Ray Hughes Gallery and this was a turning point for you.

Ray Hughes (1946–2017) was an art dealer and gallery owner. He was an influential figure in the Australian art community for more than 45 years. Hughes was one of the key people who introduced contemporary Chinese art to Australian audiences.

WANG: Yes. Ray Hughes Gallery was one of the few galleries in Sydney that accepted Chinese artists.

ZU: How did he discover you?

WANG: It wasn't really that he found me. Claire Roberts took me to see him. I brought some pictures of my work.

ZU: That was a very important recommendation. How many shows did you have at Ray Hughes? Did you sell well?

WANG: Two, held two years apart. It was pretty good. The National Gallery of Australia acquired seven pieces of 'Two from One' metal works from my show. Judith [Neilson] bought about ten works.

ZU: Did Ray Hughes get involved in what you created?

WANG: No. Not at all. He was very hands off. I must say Ray Hughes was a fantastic dealer. Every Saturday, artists and collectors would gather at his gallery, eating and drinking. He really enjoyed these get-togethers, whether it was to exchange ideas or just social networking.

This was in the 90s, before the internet. There was much discussion of dreams and desires.

ZU: That's right. Visiting galleries was an important activity in many people's lives.

WANG: The second exhibition was my SCA master's graduation work. There were 40 pieces. Ray Hughes didn't show the works at his gallery but he liaised with collectors. Queensland Art Gallery [and Gallery of Modern Art] acquired this series of works.

ZU: What was the reason you left Ray Hughes?

WANG: Because I went to back to Beijing. I hardly ever come back to Sydney.

ZU: That shouldn't be a problem. You could still have a gallery representing you in Sydney.

WANG: When I had a gallery, there were pressures. It was subtle. Creating work made them like consumer goods, made for sale. Somehow, it ended up I didn't want to do it anymore.

ZU: You wanted to make art just for yourself. Not as a job.

WANG: That's right. Precisely!

ZU: It is publicly known that you helped Judith Neilson set up White Rabbit Gallery. Wasn't that also a difficult task in the sense of choosing what to purchase?

The White Rabbit Gallery, which was established in 2009 in Sydney, holds the world's largest collection of 21st century Chinese contemporary art.

WANG: Art is not the way Judith makes money. She just wants to do a good job. It's very simple. For this reason, I was under no pressure when I helped her choose works. I didn't need to worry if the work would increase in value.

ZU: Did you receive a commission from artist if a deal was made?

WANG: Never.

ZU: When you worked together, what was the focus, the criteria when you chose a work?

WANG: Well, if you ask Judith, she would say, 'that I like it.' From my point of view, I also needed to like it. We agreed that if she was to buy something, we must both like the same work. It was never only one of us who chose.

Judith not only has money, but she also has the very rare faculty of appreciation, of taste. She didn't need me to suggest anything. She could do it on her own. I led the way because she didn't know where to go.

ZU: Leading the way was crucial, especially when she first came to Beijing. But to be able to let go is also very important for one's own creativity, I believe.

WANG: That's right.

ZU: Let's talk about your creative work. Do you think Australia has had any impact on you?

WANG: Definitely!

For us, our art is our world and our world is our experience. I lived in Sydney for ten years, not in New York. Everything planted a seed in me during the time I spent in Sydney. My work includes and reflects all those characteristics, appearances and sensibility.

I want to make a statement.

ZU: Go ahead ...

WANG: The work I created was in fact my understanding of my time and myself. When I say 'myself', I mean the society I lived in, the people I engaged with, the books I read, the knowledge I absorbed, even the food I ate – all of these made me. My work is about society. How much of this I captured in my work is a product of how extensively I perceived the world.

ZU: Your art closely reflects social phenomena. And because of that, you succeeded in 2000. The public responded to your work. Since then, have you always retained a clear vision in regard to your practice?

WANG: Last year, a Milan publisher produced a book putting together nearly 20 years of my work, including those I spent creating in Australia. Of course, this made me reflect on my practice. As artists, we must constantly engage in self-reflection.

I have always tried to create something true. I question the truths I have always believed in. Sometimes we fool ourselves. We think the work expresses truth, but if we think carefully, there may be unconscious egotistical undercurrents coming through in the artistic expression. We have very high expectations, we want to tell the viewers something.

ZU: Or to make a comment?

WANG: Yes. The intention is not to look down on others. 'Look at me. I am superior and I want to tell you how things are.' I have doubts, I lack belief…

ZU: This sort of self-doubt is rare.

WANG: I have major doubts!

ZU: Are you contradicting yourself?

WANG: Absolutely. I reject myself completely. I am standing on the threshold of farewelling the past so that I can start again.

So when you asked me what I am working on, to be honest, I do not know, I'm in the fray…

ZU: That's totally understandable to me.

WANG: There are two factors operating here. First, I think that because of the great expansion of social media, there are no longer any surprises. And creating surprise is the crux of our creative work, don't you agree?

ZU: From the viewers' point of view, yes, absolutely.

WANG: It is essential. Without it there's no point in making the work. Are you still trying to pretend? I don't want to pretend. I have no more surprises to show you. Nothing!

The skills we learnt were to create a sense of surprise, 'Look, you painted something so lifelike! Look at the eyes, the jewellery, the skin.' And when you move from realism to abstraction, you say, 'Look at that deformation, how brave was that!' or 'Put your shit in a jar and sell it as jam.' Isn't this the way it goes?

Secondly, over the last three decades, the growing disparity between rich and poor has caused a social crisis. We feel it regardless of whether we have money or not. Petit bourgeois sentiment is a pretence. It's just fine to listen to Mozart and drink wine. Everyone is fine, we decay together. Who cares? But when there are different levels [in society] ... I get annoyed just thinking about it. Do you have a problem or not? What do you have? You have money? Dammit! [speaks animatedly]

ZU: How about art? It doesn't disappoint you, does it?

WANG: [sighs] Art too! It's not art that makes me disappointed. It's the current art scene that annoys me.

ZU: Are you planning a big show in the next a couple of years?

WANG: I will make some new works. But I won't make huge works in the next few years. I have a studio in 798 in Beijing. That's more than enough.

ZU: Do you have many followers in Beijing who like your work?

WANG: No. It's just the people in the circle, the insiders. I think there are very few people who like contemporary art in China compared with those in Europe and America.

ZU: Last question. Are there many people in China who know about Australian art?

WANG: Very few.

But Australia isn't the only place they don't know about. It's the same for art from other countries – Spain, New Zealand, Canada – even France. If you ask a Chinese person about art, except for some famous artists, they do not understand.

ZU: Are they interested?

WANG: The reality is that, even today, in large part, China has retained its preference for the traditional, such as *guohua* (ink painting). Modern and contemporary art are still, in many respects, alien forms. However, due to an exponential increase in cultural exchanges and the circulation of information, the younger generation has a growing appreciation of modern and contemporary art.

ZU: Based on my observations, contemporary art in China is merely a fashionable trend – it is not embedded within society. It seems very similar to the 1980s, when we first encountered Western modernism. It cannot compete with Chinese art, which has a history of over 3,000 years and is deeply rooted in Chinese custom and tradition. Having said that, I think any change is good.

In that context, what challenges do you experience today when making art?

WANG: At present, as an artist, we are first faced with China's 'self-media' era – everyone can use social media to express themselves. We need to redefine who is the artist and rethink what an artist does. As a result, any change of form or style, regardless of whether it occurs in China or around the world, has lost its significance. I think that the urgent priority is to ask who you make this work for? Who are your viewers?

I have ended the conversation here but the recording continues with the sort back and forth exchange of ideas that artists like Wang Zhiyuan and I often have. Our discussion continued to address questions of contemporary art because we are constantly responding to and commenting on new problems and social phenomena.

'I ran away from Australia … to make art'

Conversation with Lin Chunyan
12 January 2018

Lin Chunyan (b. 1962), a self-taught painter, was born in Beijing. He started painting at a young age. His neighbour, Wu Dazhi, an art history professor from the Academy of Arts and Design of Tsinghua University (former the Central Academy of Craft Art), gave him his first introduction to fine art. At primary school, he learnt how to draw and paint from Zhao Yanchao, an art teacher at Haidian District Children's activity centre (*shaonian gong*) He often painted landscapes at the Old Summer Palace (Yuanming Yuan), the ruins of the Imperial Gardens that were destroyed in 1860 during the second Opium War. In autumn, the Old Summer Palace attracts hundreds of artists who paint the golden leaves, the white bark of the trees and the colonial columns. Lin painted there because he lived close by. From 1981 to 1984, Lin Chunyan moved around, painting in central and northern China, including Wuhan Donghu, Hubei; Baoji, Shaanxi; Guangzhou, Guangdong; and Acheng, Harbin.

In 1989, Lin was invited to an artist-in-residency program at the Tasmanian School of Art, Hobart. In 1994 he graduated with honours from the Faculty of Visual and Performing Art of Western Sydney University after one year's study with his supervisor David Hull, the Dean of the Faculty.

Lin Chunyan currently lives in Beijing and works as a professional artist. His studio is located in Songzhuang, home to many other artists' studios.

I had heard about Lin Chunyan from Guan Wei and Ah Xian, who participated in the University of Tasmania's artist-in-residency program together with him in 1989. Many other mutual friends had also mentioned him. I was curious to hear his story. I introduced myself to him through social media –

WeChat – explaining this project to him. This conversation took place via video call on 12 January 2018.

ZU: I have heard your name often in the past two years since I started writing this book. I am glad that I finally got in touch with you. I would like to talk to you about your art and your Australian experience.

What effect did the art-in-residency at the Tasmanian School of Art have on you?

LIN: It gave me encouragement and confidence. I never had any art training. I was an ordinary painter in Beijing. While I was at art school, I visited the library all the time, absorbing new information. The students and campus life, lectures by international artists – all of that had a huge impact on me.

I didn't encounter much from the perspective of cultural exchange because I couldn't communicate in English.

ZU: What happened after you completed your artist-in-residency in 1989?

LIN: I didn't come back to China. My sister was in America. She sent me US$3,000 and suggested I stay longer. I used that money to attend a course studying English.

ZU: Were you able to paint during that time?

LIN: I had one exhibition at EMR Galleries (1990) and sold one painting.

When I was in China, since the age of 19, I only painted. I did nothing else. When I came to Sydney, I repaired gas stoves, delivered mail, drove a taxi, worked as an off-set printer, worked in a juice store, installed window lights, laid bricks and did construction work.

ZU: That's a lot of different skills. You must be a very fast learner.

LIN: [laughs] If you're a painter with no formal training, you can do anything with your hands.

ZU: How long did you work like this?

LIN: It lasted about five years. We were all together, we artists, as friends. Everyone's situation was hard. But although life was hard, we still saw each other and people like Mabel [Lee]. We drank together.

Then I went back to Beijing.

ZU: Australia has an environment of creative freedom, yet you didn't stay.

LIN: Life was too hard. I was worried that I might never be able to paint again. But in China there were opportunities. That's the only reason I came back. I ran away from Australia because I wanted to continue to make art.

It doesn't matter where we are, we are all still making art. That's very important to me.

ZU: How was it when you returned to Beijing?

LIN: A lot better. I knew many people. I had more space. I could travel to other provinces to meet old friends. I found my place.

ZU: Geoff Raby said you painted some real Australian landscapes when you lived on the outskirts of southern Sydney, at Bundeena.

LIN: I painted in Bundeena for two years, between 2004 and 2006. I rented a studio near Shen Jiawei's house.

ZU: Did you paint like an impressionist?

LIN: No. I took a lot of photos. I could see the landscape from my window.

ZU: Where are the paintings?

LIN: I brought them back to Beijing. Most were sold through Geoff [Raby]. Many of the collectors are Australians. About 50 per cent went back to Australia.

ZU: That's interesting.

LIN: So strange. [laughs]

ZU: When you painted them, did you feel anything special?

LIN: To be honest. I didn't feel much at all. I used wax mixed with oil. The effect looked like Chinese landscape painting.

ZU: But it seems to me that people bought them and brought it back to Australia, because they connect the painting to this place, don't you think.

LIN: Hmmm ...

ZU: When you returned to Beijing, did your new paintings reflect Australia – your memories of the place?

LIN: They're about the relationship between me and nature. My landscapes are realistic, but the person is blurred, out of focus. The character is not real, like in a dream.

ZU: Is there a reason for that? You often depict people crashing to each other. Why's that? And they're all upside down!

LIN: [laughs] I don't know why! Perhaps it's something about my brain.

I had open heart surgery when I was eight years old. I always feel uncomfortable when anyone in my paintings is upright. I blame the blood transfusion I received. It made me ... I can't explain ... but I think it changed me a lot.

ZU: Do you turn the canvas around to paint?

LIN: No. I paint it the right way round.

ZU: Do you think there might be any influence from when you lived in Australia?

LIN: I think so. When I lived in Tasmania, there was a small bay, people swam there naked. It was so mysterious.

ZU: Your paintings remind me of Sidney Nolan's work. Nolan was one of the first artists who went to China.

LIN: My graduation essay was written about him.

ZU: Ah! How interesting.

After the conversation, I asked Lin to send me his writing. Lin's essay analyses Nolan's paintings – themes, style and technique, and especially their unique Australian characteristics and psychological states. He is also interested the relationship between artists and society.

LIN: And Author Boyd.

ZU: Your paintings don't show the hardship you experienced in Australia. You use a lot of grey tones, but there are bright highlights.

LIN: The reason for grey is that before, when I was in Beijing, it was truly grey. It contrasted with the red walls. It stimulated me. The upside-down person in my painting depicts a sense of freedom.

ZU: And happiness too.

LIN: Yes. It's a sensation between dream and reality.

ZU: Painting are much neglected in contemporary art. Do you agree?

LIN: Nature has its cycles. So does art.

ZU: Do you mean that in time, more attention will be paid to painting?

LIN: I don't know. It's possible.

ZU: The size of your paintings has increased. Before, you painted small canvases; now they are over two metres long.

LIN: When I painted at the scene, the canvas had to be small, otherwise it was hard to move with wet paint. When I'm in the studio, I like to paint life-size – not too large. That way it's more real.

ZU: So you didn't intend to attract more attention by painting on a larger scale.

LIN: No. Not at all.

ZU: Many artists have stopped painting. Why have you continued?

LIN: Art is a religion to me. It seems that I have been summoned to paint till the end.

ZU: In recent years, there have been more and more contemporary art installations and works with an emphasis on audio-visual and new media, but you have focused on painting.

LIN: That's because I still have something to say. I am still expressing myself through my paintings.

ZU: Hmmm.

LIN: I know it is a very narrow road, but I also know the road is there, although it entails great effort and difficulty.

ZU: Perhaps it is narrower. You have been painting for many years. For you, I would imagine, it is also a matter of depth. You want to explore more deeply.

LIN: The language of painting hasn't been fully expressed, I mean.

ZU: For you as an oil painter, what is the connection between oil painting and Chinese art?

LIN: For me, the medium makes no difference. Chinese landscape is about the relationships between human beings and nature. I express my observation and contemplations about this relationship, only using a different medium.

ZU: That makes sense.

Thank you so much for taking the time to talk with me. I look forward to meeting you in person one day.

Though short, the conversation with Lin Chunyan was important because he provides readers with a sense of how it feels to be an artist, regardless of external conditions.

The Queensland Art Gallery and Gallery of Modern Art has two Lin Chunyan's paintings, 'Two figures climbing a tree'

(1985) and 'Self portrait – Opening the door' (1989). They were gift of Nicholas Jose and Claire Roberts through the Queensland Art Gallery Foundation 2008, donated through the Australian Government's Cultural Gifts Program.

On 12 May 2018, I finally met Lin Chunyan in his studio at Song Zhuang during my visit to Beijing. Viewing his original paintings in his studio helped me to understand his outpouring of creativity and his inseparable relationship with painting. He paints with tree branches instead of paint brushes, a direct relationship between him and nature.

'Definitely contemporary Chinese art'

Conversation with Shen Shaomin
17 DECEMBER 2017

Shen Shaomin (b.1956) is a self-taught contemporary artist who grew up in Acheng, Heilongjiang province. Shen began his art career painting Cultural Revolution posters. His interest in printmaking was partly influenced by his father, who was a skilled carpenter. In the mid-1980s Shen became a professional artist. He soon started to explore experimental art. In 1989 he came to Sydney, where he lived for ten years. In 2001 Shen returned to his homeland to continue his art making.

Today, Shen is one of the most recognised contemporary artists in the world. In 2010 he participated in the 17th Biennale of Sydney. The following year he had a solo exhibition, 'The Day After Tomorrow', at 4A Centre for Contemporary Asian Art. In a further engagement with Australia to promote cultural exchange and understanding, he opened up his Beijing studio in 2012 as a residence to support young Australian artists.

I met Shen Shaomin briefly in 2011 at 4A Centre for Contemporary Asian Art where he had a solo exhibition. In March 2017 I told him about this book. He was very supportive, providing information and answering my queries. I said I'd visit him in person for a conversation.

On 17 December 2017, I flew to Guangzhou from Beijing. Shen has a studio in Redtory Art District. It was nearly 7 o'clock when I arrived because my flight was delayed by about two hours. Shen and two assistants were waiting patiently for me. Shen showed me his studio. The front room has a computer work station, a study corner, with his work plans framed and displayed on the walls. The main room is a huge open space. His 'Standard Portraits' series were on the floor. On the wall hung mixed-media works by Shen Shaomin's daughter. In the corner were weights and exercise machines.

ZU: Shall we do the interview first?

SHEN: No. Let's eat first. It's more important.

Ah Long, Shen's assistant, cooked for us. While I was waiting, the other assistant put on a documentary film for me to watch. It was Shen Shaomin's recent exhibition 'There is no problem', curated by David Elliott, the artistic director for the 17th Biennale of Sydney when Shen was in the exhibition in 2010.

We had diner at Shen's studio. His neighbour, also an artist, came over to join us. We caught up a little, telling each other our common friends' movements. After dinner, we started our conversation in his study corner.

ZU: Tell me about yourself.

SHEN: I was born in *dongbei* [the northeast], the birthplace of the Manchu Dynasty, in the Acheng district of Harbin. My mother is a Manchu.

ZU: Really? So you are not Hanzuren [ethnically Chinese]. [grins]

SHEN: Half-half. [smiles back]

ZU: When did you start to make art?

I quickly realised Shen Shaomin is very reticent when it comes to talking about himself. He didn't tell me anything voluntarily unless I insisted on getting to the bottom of the matter. I have combined some of my questions and Shen's answers together to make it easier for readers to follow.

SHEN: I have never been to art school but I've liked art since I was a child. I liked to draw. When I was 17, I left school and took over my father's job after he passed away.

ZU: What kind of job was that?

SHEN: First, I was assigned to a textile factory. It was a big company in the northeast. The factory had tens of thousands of workers, all female. I didn't feel it was the right job for a man, so I didn't go. After that, I did some casual work.

ZU: What kind of casual work?

SHEN: I applied for a temporary job in a brick factory, writing slogans.

During the Cultural Revolution, political slogans and posters were everywhere. Writing slogans was a full-time job. Popular slogans included Chairman Mao's quotations and exhortations to fight capitalism, praise communism, and carry the great revolution through to the end. Those ten years of slogans were overwhelming, deafening, and in people's eyes every day. Everyone's emotions were affected.

Then came an opportunity. A film distribution company was recruiting artists. I applied for the job. I remember I didn't sleep for two or three days so that I could practise painting with gouache. Now everything's done by inkjet, but in those days, it was all done by hand. I practised and practised ... I came first in the exam.

ZU: That's great! How many did they take on?

SHEN: Actually, they only needed one. [smiles]

For five years from 1975, I worked in the publicity section of a film distribution company where I painted movie and film posters. I also worked as a projectionist.

ZU: That was a valuable experience. I miss those projectors.

> *I happened to grow up in film studios because my mother was a documentary film director at the Central Studio of News Reels Production.*

SHEN: [lights a cigarette] Then I was transferred to a newly built movie theatre. It was very modern. I worked there for another ten years painting movie posters. It made me a very competent realistic painter. I did quite well there, painting large-scale works with big flat-head brushes.

At the same time, I started experimenting with woodcut prints. Acheng had a printmaking group.

> *Acheng Printmaking Group began in the 1960s. It was influenced by the Great Northern Wilderness prints depiction of the unique scenery and the strong rustic atmosphere of the northern countryside.*

It was a very important group of artists. I was one of the three organisers. We taught some students.

> *In 1984 a print by Shen Shaomin was selected and shown at the sixth National Fine Arts Exhibition at the National Art Museum of China. The exhibition, held every five years, was regarded as representing work of the highest standard. It was the largest national government art exhibition in China. Because of his achievement, Shen was promoted to the Acheng Print Academy.*

I became the youngest professional artist in Heilongjiang. I received honours, I was paid above the fixed salary rate and won an award as one of the eight top talents. [laughs]

I was given further opportunities. I could go to Beijing to see exhibitions using work expenses. I started to open my eyes to contemporary art.

ZU: I see. The eighties was a really exciting time. Artists were actively experimenting with varied artistic expressions. It was also chaotic. I was still a student at CAFA. I remember our lecturers didn't know how to teach us any more. [laughs] On the one hand, they were trying out new things themselves, but on the other hand, they had to teach the same old syllabus. Contemporary art was definitely not on the syllabus.

SHEN: No. It wasn't.

I went to Beijing and met Lin Chunyan and Guan Wei, as well as poets, Yang Lian, Mang Ke, Hei Dachun and some rock stars. From that time, I changed my views about art.

I reexamined the art I made and realised it wasn't art. It was propaganda. So I resigned in 1987.

I lived in Beijing for two years. I saw more things and met many people. At that time, making contemporary art was semi-underground. There was nowhere to exhibit – non-realistic painting was regarded as bourgeois liberalism. The only possibilities were showing at foreign embassies and foreigners' homes. I had shows and sold a few works to make a living.

ZU: Ha! Selling paintings to foreigners was quite exciting, wasn't it? I remember when I sold my paintings to a Japanese collector, I felt a kind of excitement that my art was dialoguing with the world. Now, looking back, that was probably merely an illusion.

I was intrigued that although Shen's path had been completely different from mine, many of our experiences were shared.

How do you see the art that you made in 1989 today? When did your personal artistic style begin to form?

SHEN: [lights another cigarette] It was at that time that my art matured. I used the printmaking form but my prints weren't traditional woodcut prints. I used textile dyeing and printing methods to make the works. The principles of the process were very similar. I carved the patterns on the drum and then printed the colour separations. This technique produced a print as well as a soft sculpture. I made a lot of works with this method. That was the transition period. From there, I turned to installation and making three-dimensional contemporary art.

ZU: Hmmm. That's the advantage of a lack of restriction from academy education!

SHEN: Yes. There are no boundaries.

ZU: In 1989 you came to Australia as a visiting scholar. Then you came back again, didn't you?

SHEN: Yes. In 1989, I visited Sydney with other members of the Acheng Print Academy. An Australian printmaking forum invited us to participate in a print exhibition in Canberra and the Australian National University. In Melbourne we gave a lecture. We moved around and looked at things for a month.

The second time I came to Australia was different. It was an artists' residency program. Guan Wei, Ah Xian and Lin Chunyan went to Tasmania and I went to Western Sydney University. Zhou Si organised this for us when he was cultural counsellor.

Shen Shaomin first met Nicholas Jose (Zhou Si) in 1987 at the Acheng Print Academy.

I came back to Beijing in April. I started to prepare for a three-man show at the Red Gate Gallery that had been planned before I went to Australia. It was actually the gallery before the Red Gate, at the Beijing Ancient Observatory.

ZU: Ah. Wasn't that Brian Wallace's gallery?

SHEN: Yes. That's him. He organised the show but he didn't have a gallery then. He used to borrow spaces to show the works.

The opening of our exhibition was very close to June Fourth. Students had already started the processions in the streets. So, although many people came to see the exhibition, especially many foreigners, it was forced to close after a day and a half.

ZU: Oh. That's really bad.

As far as I know from our previous talks, you came to Sydney after the post-89 psychological trauma, but the ten years you spent in Sydney didn't go very well. What were your most direct and deepest impressions of Australia?

SHEN: Going abroad for the first time, everything felt very new. But at the same time, I noticed Australians didn't know about China in any meaningful way. For example, a journalist interviewed me asking very general questions. They were more interested in ideological things, for example what we thought of Mao Zedong. I remember I answered, 'Mao is an artist! [raises his right arm, saluting] Wasn't he a performing artist?' I like making jokes. [smiles]

[lowers his arm and picks up another cigarette] Perhaps Australians only had a superficial knowledge of China because that's all the media reported on. They even asked if any Chinese still wear pigtails. [laughs]

ZU: Ha ha!

In the interview you did with Wu Hong, you commented that your Australian experience provided a global perspective for your art practice. Do you think your work was strengthened because of its cross-cultural context? I think that would have been a hard-earned gain but a big one for you.

What also interested me was the experience behind your work. It largely comments on power, on distorted forms, and on your obsessive interest in life and death. Where did the framework for these ideas come from?

SHEN: [lights the cigarette and exhales slowly] There was no particular experience. Perhaps one influence on me was witnessing my father's and grandmother's death at a young age. I realised that people die. I thought about it often.

Freedom is what I seek in life. Whatever I do, freedom is the essence of independent thinking and creation. Bonsai represents a distortion of nature.

ZU: I agree.

How did you deal with Sydney – the unfamiliar environment – when you arrived?

SHEN: Any experience has an impact on making art. For example, there was not much creative freedom in China. People were longing for Western freedom.

ZU: Did you feel free when you arrived in Australia?

SHEN: There were new problems. You had spiritual freedom, but you were limited by economic conditions so you couldn't finish your work. That's another kind of restriction. My experience had taught me that there's no absolute freedom.

ZU: Exactly!

In 2002, you left Sydney at the peak of your creativity. Why?

SHEN: I was working on several projects. One of them was the bone project. I developed the plan in Sydney but the Australian government had very strict animal protection laws, which made it impossible to obtain the necessary funding to realise such a large-scale work.

ZU: So you had to leave Sydney?

SHEN: Yes. Many people couldn't understand why I gave up such a good environment. I remember I replied, 'I cannot live just by breathing fresh air.'

> Shen Shaomin returned to his home town in 2002 and continued making art. In 2007, he had four major solo exhibitions in China, curated by Wu Hong: 'Project No. 1: Tiananmen Reconstruction', 'Kowtow Pump', the 'Bonsai' series, and 'Fighter–X'. These attracted lots of attention. These works highlighted Shen's unique artistic sensibilities. They were recognised as his most personal and ideologically mature work to date.

> In 2010, he presented 'G5 Summit' at the 17th Biennale of Sydney as a Chinese artist. The following year, he exhibited a site-specific installation, 'The Day After Tomorrow', at the 4A Centre for Contemporary Asian Art in Sydney.

ZU: The artists' residency program you set up in your Beijing studio was a great outcome after your 4A show.

SHEN: Yes. Both Aaron [Seeto] and I had the same idea and motivation. We talked about it. I felt that Australians lacked understanding about China. I wanted to provide opportunities for Australian artists to get to know Chinese artists at a deeper level – for example, to get to know how they work and to develop closer communication. Many Australian artists have never been to China. The people who came were mostly tourists. They had no idea about what was happening in contemporary Chinese art.

I happened to have a huge studio. I don't really need all the space. Because each of my works is different, I don't have ongoing assistants. Once a project starts, I make the work wherever it can be made. So the studio is only for planning projects. I wanted to utilise the spare space for the artists' residency program.

ZU: Your artists' residency program has been well received in Australia. More and more artists are familiar with your name because of applying for this program each year.

SHEN: Really? I've hardly been back so I wouldn't know. Anyway, it is one way to keep my connection with Australia.

I have always supported young artists. We have a work-sharing activity twice a year – three Australian artists, three Chinese artists – where we project each artist's work onto a screen and have a group discussion. I arrange interviews for them.

One month is very short. I suggest to them that they don't try to make any works. The main purpose is looking around and communicating with Chinese artists. They can check out the farmers' markets, for example. We have volunteers to take them around. We have translators. Many artists like to come.

ZU: Of course.

In 2012, Claire Roberts curated 'Go Figure! Contemporary Chinese Portraiture'. Your 'Standard Portrait – Mao Zedong' showed at the Sherman Contemporary Art Foundation. Did she get in touch with you?

SHEN: The work was in [Uli] Sigg's collection but initially they were not going to show this work. First the plan was to show Mao Zedong's body [from the G5 Summit]. This didn't get approval from the Australian government because they were concerned that the Chinese government might protest. So Claire talked to me about changing Mao's portrait to one with a soft frame so that can never be displayed straight no matter how you hang it. The *Sydney Morning Herald* interviewed me about the Mao body work. It was a full-page article with Ai Weiwei and my picture on the front. But they didn't show the work.

ZU: It was a sensitive topic.

SHEN: Claire asked me and I said I didn't mind.

ZU: Did you come to see the show? Did you like it?

SHEN: I didn't come to the opening but I gave a talk at Gene's. The exhibition title, 'Xiangxiang' is excellent. Claire is an experienced China hand. She understands Chinese. Another person wouldn't have come up with this name.

ZU: Indeed. It's a clever pun in Chinese, just like the English title, 'Go Figure'.

A feature of your work is its large scale. Naturally that costs a lot. Who is your financial supporter?

SHEN: To date, I'm not represented by a gallery. I have collaborations with galleries. I show them my proposals and if they are interested, they commission me to make the work, and they sell the work. For example, Beijing Tang Contemporary Art, Platform China Contemporart Art Institute (Beijing), Courtyard Gallery and Hong Kong Osage Gallery. People invest in me to make works.

ZU: It's a risky investment because, from my understanding, to realise the actual work from your proposal requires a huge amount of money.

SHEN: That's true.

Sometimes a gallery invites me to do an exhibition. I come up with an idea, they provide the funding, and they manage the whole show.

ZU: There were some comments about your G5 Summit at Art Basel Hong Kong (2017). It seemed that they singled you out as a Chinese contemporary artist. What is your view on this? Do you think being a Chinese contemporary artist is a unique position or a limitation?

SHEN: Errrr … [pause] Contemporary art is too broad. Definitely contemporary Chinese art. It has its uniqueness. We have unique social problems, systems, concerns and overall cultural background.

ZU: So you don't reject the title? A lot of Chinese artists do not like to be positioned as Chinese artists.

SHEN: Of course not. There's no point in rejecting it. And it's not important. Whether they put Chinese in front of your name or not, you are a Chinese artist! I have an Australian passport, but I am still Chinese. You are Chinese in your bones.

ZU: Do you feel it is an advantage to be a Chinese artist in the global contemporary art scene?

SHEN: Not particularly. China is behind in contemporary art compared with the Western world. Yet, China is a focus for the world as well. Many people follow Chinese contemporary art because China pays close attention to its own interests – and it is very volatile. Because of that, for a period of time, contemporary Chinese artists were in the spotlight too.

ZU: How about now?

SHEN: It is impossible to be in the forefront forever. For example, [British curator] David [Elliott] is now investigating Russian contemporary art.

ZU: Do you think there's been a shift in attention? Would that affect what you make?

SHEN: You can't expect everyone to look only in one place. That's not my business. In 2008, the Chinese art market declined because of the global financial crisis. Many said that the basis for the Chinese art market would collapse. But

I didn't care. In the 1980s, there was neither a market nor a platform for it, and yet we still made art. I don't participate in auctions so the market has no direct impact on me.

In the beginning, no one wanted to invest on my work so I sold my house to make work.

ZU: That was a risk.

SHEN: I'm afraid I am ruthless if I want to do something. [smiles] I come back whenever I want to.

ZU: Oh dear!

SHEN: Also, not everyone can buy my work. First they are big, and secondly, they are not designed to be pleasing to display in your home. [smiles] They mainly go to gallery collections.

The art market is important for some artists, but it's not crucial to me.

ZU: 'Art history' was exhibited in the Busan Biennale 2016. How did audiences respond to it?

SHEN: The work had a great response from the public. To me, it was a way to cancel all the definitions about what art is. Art attracts people's attention precisely because it cannot be defined.

ZU: 2015 seems to have been a turning point for your art practice. You combined poetry with your art.

SHEN: It is not that I combined poetry with my art. Poetry is one of the forms of creation. Poetry is my new art form. When I do not select any other materials, I choose text. I can make work with it. It is the same.

ZU: Compared with your massive works, this is a minimalist approach. Is this your intention?

SHEN: No. It's more that at that moment, I felt that I could express myself more directly with poetry, so I used it. My poems have a philosophical intent; their meaning cannot be expressed fully by an installation or a sculpture. Poetry is more accurate.

ZU: I see your poetry has an English version. It reads very well.

SHEN: Archibald [McKenzie] did the translation. He collects my work. We are very good friends.

ZU: How do you see Australia now?

SHEN: I miss it. I have many friends there. It's just that I'm too busy to go back. I've experienced many things in life, my broken marriages … but I am an optimist, a positive pessimist. [smiles] You've got to live, whatever happens. Life goes on … I do whatever I have to …

Australia provided me with the opportunity to see more. It gave me a broader vision. It makes a difference when creating works for people who have had experiences living overseas. For example, when I had just come back, many artists were using demolition symbols in their work. They were concerned about what was happening around them.

ZU: Talking about symbols, your poems are in Chinese? The language is a very symbolic form, isn't it?

SHEN: Poems are very difficult to translate, but it is my language. I normally show them in both languages, Chinese and English.

ZU: What's a typical day for you?

SHEN: I normally exercise in the morning. I go for a ten-kilometre run at about 7 o'clock along the river. After breakfast, I reply to emails and texts, then do weights. I start working at 11 o'clock.

From beginning to end, Shen Shaomin was highly engaged with our dialogue. His discourse was very sincere and clearly demonstrated his support for my project. Obviously, he wasn't able to be entirely candid about certain topics and details and I fully comprehend his reasons for this. He left me with more questions to contemplate – queries about fragility, the unpredictable future, the role an artist plays, the persona of a hero and sacrifices. All of these are yet to be examined through the art-making process, but it is not clear at what cost.

Chapter IV

Giving birth and nourishing,
having without possessing,
acting with no expectations,
leading and not trying to control:
this is the supreme virtue.

Lao-tzu, *Tao Te Ching*, Chapter 10

Continuity

This chapter contains five conversations I had with curator Claire Roberts, gallery directors Brian Wallace and Aaron Seeto, and art collectors Geoff Raby and John Yu. It traces their work – independent of each other, but sometimes connected to the same artists – that made it possible for Australians to access contemporary Chinese art created from the late 1990s to the present. Each dialogue gives readers a different perspective yet, taken together, they demonstrate Australian society's visual engagement with Chinese art. In some cases the collaborations were successful, while others were found lacking in some way.

I have constructed this chapter with a multi-focal approach, each one discussing contemporary Chinese art, or Asian art more broadly, from a separate angle. Each narrative is an in-depth response to the challenges these individuals encountered.

The questions I was seeking answers to were, first, in what way have contemporary Chinese artists been presented to Australia? Secondly, what justifications were made by the curators, gallery directors and collectors when contemporary Chinese art was introduced to Australian audiences? And finally, whether the visual engagement has been sufficient for people to experience and understand China through its art, culture and aesthetics.

To arrive at an all-embracing encounter with what is implicit in all these experiences, for the final time, I tossed three coins and inquired of the *I Ching*: Ultimately, China and Australia need each other, in the same way as contemporary art and society are reliant on each other. Yet they are mutually exclusive according to the law of nature – they embody the interplay of yin and yang. How can two polarities achieve independence and mutual dependence? When society is harmonious and people are content, will art naturally disappear?

I found an answer in hexagram 29, *Kan*, The Abyss (Water).

ABOVE: THE ABYSS, WATER
BELOW: THE ABYSS, WATER

This is one of the four most important hexagrams in the first part of the *I Ching*. Both creative and receptive, it repeats the symbol of danger, a double jeopardy. As an image, it represents water coming from above and below, from heaven and earth. Wilhelm translates:

> THE JUDGMENT
> The Abyss repeated,
> If you are sincere, you have success in your heart,
> And whatever you do succeeds.
>
> Through repeatedly facing danger we grow accustomed to it. Water sets the example for the right conduct under such circumstances. It flows on and on, and merely fills up all the places through which it flows; it does not shrink from any dangerous spot nor from any plunge, and nothing can make it lose its own essential nature. It remains true to itself under all conditions. In the same way, if one is sincere when confronted with difficulties, the heart can penetrate the meaning of the situation. ... naturally that is the action we should take to succeed.

The *Kan* hexagram combines Confucianism and Taoism, the former emphasising the creative yang energy, which can be understood as society. The latter pays attention to the receptive yin energy/water, which can be perceived as art. If nature experiences recurring hardship, acting sincerely will bring peace out of chaos. As the *I Ching* advises, thoroughly and persistently carrying out what has to be done will bring success. Art and society will always be in a relationship, like water that flows and lasts infinitely.

I am gratefully satisfied with the image of the *Kan* hexagram – that is, the importance of positive energy in the midst of negative energy. The people I had these dialogues with have maintained a low profile, and their stories are unheard. However, because of their sincerity and whole-heartedness, they have entered a realm of fulfilment.

A very hands-on Chinese art curator

Conversation with Claire Roberts
3 April 2017

Dr Claire Roberts (b. 1959) is a curator and a historian of modern and contemporary Chinese art. She is an Australian Research Council Future Fellow and Associate Professor of Art History at the University of Melbourne. Claire is fluent in Mandarin. She studied at Beijing Languages Institute (1978–79) and the Central Academy of Fine Arts, Beijing (1979–81). Her PhD (2006), undertaken in the Research School of Pacific and Asian History at ANU, focused on the work of scholar, art historian and modern brush-and-ink painter Huang Binhong (1865–1955).

Claire Roberts was a pioneer in curating contemporary Chinese art in Australian art museums. In 1992, she curated 'New Art from China: Post-Mao Product', which was exhibited at the Art Gallery of NSW, the Queensland Art Gallery and other venues. Then she was a curatorial adviser on Chinese art for the Asia–Pacific Triennial of Contemporary Art, Queensland Art Gallery, Brisbane in 1993, 1996 and 1999.

Claire's main focus of study is modern and contemporary Chinese art and visual culture, and artistic contact and dialogue between Australia and China. In recent years she has curated exhibitions including 'Go Figure! Contemporary Chinese Portraiture' at the National Portrait Gallery (Canberra, 2012) and 'Yang Zhichao: Chinese Bible' at Sherman Contemporary Art Foundation (SCAF Project 26, 2015). She has published widely on Chinese art and visual and material culture.

The first time I met Claire Roberts was in 2010 at 'Coming and Going' (*lai-lai wang-wang*), a group exhibition I participated in. We kept in touch.

In the first week of April 2017, Claire came to Sydney for Chinese Contemporary Art Month. She was invited to be the moderator and a keynote speaker for the event. Claire and I met on 3 April at the State Library of NSW.

Naturally, our conversation began with what had just happened.

ZU: You have been closely connected to and have many insights into art in China since the 1980s. What is your view on contemporary Chinese art?

ROBERTS: I have always been interested in contemporary Chinese art but now is a different world compared to the 1970s and 1980s.

I try to keep up with things as best I can. I have been asking a lot of questions about my responses to much recent Chinese art. Today, artists are using very different artistic media and languages to express their ideas.

ZU: I agree. And these issues are entirely relevant to what we're about to explore. But let's go back to the starting point. How did you come to learn Chinese?

ROBERTS: I went to school in Melbourne. It was a private girls' school (Ivanhoe Girls' Grammar). The year I started there, at the beginning of secondary school, Chinese and French were compulsory foreign languages that everyone had to learn in first year. That was my introduction.

Australian secondary schools started to teach Chinese as a foreign language beginning in the late 1950s. It was a strategy that set out to prepare Australians for the changes to come, to understand China.

Claire talked about her school principal, Glyn France, who understood that China would be a part of Australia's future and so he phased out German and introduced Chinese, making it the first girls' school in Australia to teach Chinese.

I liked learning Chinese, so I kept going. After six years there were three of us who sat for the Higher School Certificate examination in Chinese. So, my introduction to Chinese was by chance.

ZU: In 1992, the exhibition you curated, 'Post-Mao Product: New Art from China' at the Art Gallery of NSW, was ground-breaking. When you curate a show that involves Chinese artists, do you think it is important for the curator and the artist to understand each other through the visual medium?

Post–Mao Product: New Art from China (1992–1993) was a group exhibition Claire Roberts curated with Chinese artists' works created after the China Cultural Revolution. It was first shown at the Art Gallery of NSW and toured around Australia. Artists included in the exhibition were: Chen Haiyan, Fang Lijun, He Jianguo, Lü Shengzhong, Ni Haifeng, Xu Bing and Xu Hong. A catalogue was published in association with the exhibition.

ROBERTS: I've always been a very hands-on curator. I like to establish a connection with the artists who I am considering for a show, to understand their work. I selected the artists and the works for 'New Art from China' and spent a lot of time considering the installation. If I am happy with the show then there is a good chance that the artists might be too. That exhibition was done on a tight budget. It was early days, so the artists never saw the show.

ZU: That's a shame that the artists couldn't come and see the show. But that was a difficult time too.

How about curating exhibitions with Chinese-Australian artists?

ROBERTS: An example of a particularly close collaboration with an artist was Guan Wei's 'Other Histories' exhibition at the Powerhouse Museum.

Claire Roberts was the senior curator of Asian Arts at the Powerhouse Museum (MAAS) (1988–2010). In 2006, she curated 'Other Histories: Guan Wei's Fable for a Contemporary World' for the Powerhouse Museum's Asian Gallery.

ZU: How did it come about?

ROBERTS: Guan Wei talked to me about an idea he had for a show which I really liked. It made me think about an object in the Powerhouse Museum collection, a figure of Shou Lao, the God of Longevity, which has an interesting history. The figure was discovered in Darwin in 1879. It was buried in the roots of a Banyan tree that was removed by a Chinese road gang who were contracted to clear land for a new road and eventually ended up in the Museum's collection. It seemed to me that this could be a great focal point of the exhibition.

ZU: Did Guan Wei know about it? Was it in his proposal?

ROBERTS: No. Not before I told him. But for both of us it quickly became a point of focus for the exhibition, which was Guan Wei telling his story of migration combining it with real and imagined histories of early contact between China and Australia. Through our conversation, the exhibition became much richer. Guan Wei not only painted narrative murals in the exhibition space, he also included objects from the museum's collection which became an integral part of his story telling. He assigned his own meanings to them to suit his artistic narrative.

ZU: It sounds like a double history, or a combining of history and fable.

ROBERTS: Guan Wei selected objects from the museum's collection, which were stored in the basement, to include in his display. He then wrote labels for the objects to suit his fictitious narrative – *bian gushi* [made-up stories].

ZU: Now it makes sense.

ROBERTS: But we added another layer of meaning to the labels. The actual object information was placed underneath Guan Wei's text, so people could clearly understand his playful approach to storytelling.

It was a successful exhibition and very satisfying for me as a curator, and I think for Guan Wei as an artist. It was a big project.

If I had curated the show without talking to Guan Wei, or Guan Wei had proposed and staged the exhibition without talking to me, it would have been different.

ZU: How did the public receive it?

ROBERTS: It got a lot of publicity. We allowed people to come into the gallery space to watch Guan Wei and his assistants paint the murals.

ZU: I noticed that Ah Xian's porcelain busts he made in 1998 are in the MAAS collection.

ROBERTS: Yes, there are two!

Earlier I had curated an exhibition of Ah Xian's porcelain busts at the Powerhouse. The show was also in the Asian Gallery. We included videos of Ah Xian making body casts. People were amazed by his working methods. Earlier we had selected his work for the second Asia–Pacific Triennial of Contemporary Art (APT) at the Queensland Art Gallery (1996).

Claire was one of the curatorial advisers for Chinese art for the APT2 and APT3.

ZU: Ah Xian showed at only one commercial gallery in Australia in the 1990s. That was Gene Sherman's gallery, I believe. Gene's was one of the first galleries in Sydney to show the work of Chinese artists.

ROBERTS: Yes. Gene was immediately interested in the work that was shown to her by Ah Xian, Liu Xiaoxian and Guan Wei. Gene was an emerging gallerist then. She hadn't been involved with the Irving Gallery for very long and was finding her niche. Showing works by contemporary Chinese artists was significant. Gene played an important role introducing their work to Australian audiences.

ZU: It benefited both Chinese artists and the Australian art world. It opened up new territory. How did you get involved curating contemporary Chinese art at the Sherman Contemporary Art Foundation?

ROBERTS: Gene became more and more interested in Chinese art and invited me to curate one of the shows at her gallery. Our friendship developed from there.

ZU: I would like to talk about the 'Go Figure' and 'Chinese Bible' projects that you curated.

Go Figure! Contemporary Chinese Portraiture (2012) was a joint exhibition of the National Portrait Gallery, Canberra and the Sherman Contemporary Art Foundation, Sydney. The exhibition displayed works by Chinese artists from the Sigg collection, Switzerland and the M+ Sigg collection, Hong Kong.

Chinese Bible (2009) is a major installation work by performance artist Yang Zhichao (b. 1963) comprising 3000 diaries that the artist collected over three years. The diaries' content spans fifty years of Communist China (1949–99). After the exhibition it was donated to the Art Gallery of NSW collection. In 2015, SCAF presented 'Chinese Bible' (SCAF Project 26) as part of the two-site exhibition 'Go East: The Gene & Brian Sherman Collection of Contemporary Asian Art' at the Art Gallery of NSW.

ROBERTS: For both projects, I have to thank Gene. 'Go Figure' resulted from Gene meeting Uli Sigg and deciding that she wanted to see an exhibition of the Sigg collection in Australia. So it wasn't my idea. Gene wanted to find a curator who would work on the show and asked if I'd be interested. I said yes, of course.

It is a very interesting collection. I travelled to Switzerland and met with Uli Sigg. We got on well and spent a lot of time talking. I won his confidence and was able to view everything in his collection either in the original or online.

Uli Sigg (b. 1946) was the Swiss Ambassador to China (1995–99). At that point his collection was one of the largest private collections of contemporary Chinese art in the world.

ZU: I see. I'm guessing it wasn't an easy curating task.

ROBERTS: A number of exhibitions had been curated from the Sigg collection and he had always had quite a strong hand in them. I was keen to have a … [pauses, to be sure] high degree of curatorial independence, which after long discussions he agreed to … It was quite a long process.

I worked with staff at the National Portrait Gallery in Canberra and Sherman Contemporary Art Foundation in Sydney. It was relatively quick but still it took two years.

As Gene had initiated the exhibition she wanted some major works in the exhibition to be displayed at SCAF. It was a case of one exhibition, two cities. Complicated. There were long discussions about how the two sites would work together, whether people would visit one and then the other.

In the end Sun Yuan and Peng Yu's 'Old People's Home', which required a large area and was difficult to accommodate at the National Portrait Gallery, was displayed at SCAF. In the end it all worked out and many people did manage to see both parts of the show.

ZU: The 'Chinese Bible' work requires some intellectual analysis, don't you agree? But, of course, it can be perceived poetically. The challenge was how to display or install it.

In 2015, SCAF presented 'Chinese Bible' (SCAF Project 26), an installation that formed part of 'Go East: The Gene & Brian Sherman Collection of Contemporary Asian Art'.

ROBERTS: Gene and Brian Sherman acquired 'Chinese Bible'. It was a large and important work in their collection of contemporary Asian art. Gene was keen for it to be shown at SCAF. As curator, it was up to me to work with Yang Zhichao and the SCAF team on how to stage it. The challenge was to display 3000 found Chinese diaries and make the performance installation work for an Australian audience.

I went to Beijing and met with Yang Zhichao. We got on well and talked through the installation and how to translate the content for Australian audiences.

ZU: Yes, of course. The diaries were in Chinese.

When the work was exhibited at SCAF, one component was an interactive digital installation with a selection of diaries translated into English on an iPad; an effective expansion of the original work.

ROBERTS: Yes, that was in a separate section at the rear of the gallery, behind a wall. What we came up with was a good solution – a beautiful, clean installation with the 3000 diaries displayed in a huge rectangle on a low plinth with a separate interpretive zone. Michael Moran worked closely with us to realise the concept.

Gene had seen the work displayed in a gallery in Hong Kong. You could look down from an upstairs section onto the installation of diaries. She wanted to recreate that experience, but it was not possible in the SCAF space. The ceiling wasn't high enough. There were beams. What we came up with was a good solution and in the end Yang Zhichao and Gene were very happy.

ZU: Are you saying that the curator is the boss, in this case?

ROBERTS: No, not the boss, but ... it's always complicated. You have to talk through different ideas and possibilities, and negotiate. The work of a curator is complex. You've got to keep everyone happy. You have your own vision but you need to work with the artist and the gallery to make sure the work is displayed in the best possible way.

ZU: The more I listen to you, the more I feel being an artist is easier.

ROBERTS: Communication is a big part of it. But [it's also] how you place the work in the space – artists usually have a very clear idea of how they want their work displayed. Respecting that as much as is possible is very important.

ZU: For hanging scrolls, all you need to do is to hang them on the wall, but with installations, you've got to consider the space. We talked about the concept of *yujing* the other day – the context, as you translated it. I think the curator has an important role to ensure the work speaks to the audience.

ROBERTS: It's all about teamwork. But as a curator I'm always conscious of the need to ensure that artworks are as accessible as possible to audiences. This is particularly the case if a foreign language, such as Chinese, is integral to the work.

ZU: Drawing from your own experiences, you liked the Chinese language and became good at it, you studied brush-and-ink painting in Beijing and later curated a wide variety of exhibitions. Can we talk about Yang Fudong? One of my favourite pieces is your essay on him.

> *Yang Fudong (b. 1971 Beijing) is an internationally recognised Chinese photographer best known for his films 'The Seven Sages of the Bamboo Grove' and 'No Snow on the Broken Bridge'. In 2011, Sherman Contemporary Art Foundation held an exhibition screening Yang's films using black-and-white multi-screens.*

ROBERTS: Thank you. I am particularly interested in Yang Fudong's aesthetic.

ZU: I am much drawn by his ability to connect the traditional and the contemporary. Do you think his work resonates with your perception of traditional Chinese art?

ROBERTS: I am interested in works by artists who are actively engaging with their cultural backgrounds, whatever they may be, but whose work also has a capacity to communicate more broadly, beyond that particular cultural background. The work of brush-and-ink painter Huang Binhong comes out of the Chinese landscape painting tradition. Towards the end of his life, his work became quite open; his brush strokes imbued with a real sense of energy and life. The work does not completely transcend Chineseness, but other points of contact are possible for people who are looking at the work. That is how I first responded to his paintings. You can feel the energy of his brushstrokes. That energy creates a real point of connection.

As for Yang Fudong, I think there's a lot going on in his work. What you see is not the whole picture. There are so many layers to his work, and depth. For example, his photographs and films reference old black-and-white movies from the 1920s and 30s as well as poetry and ink painting. He is a sensitive artist. I really enjoyed talking with him. I am always fascinated to meet artists.

ZU: I remember I went to see his 'No Snow on the Broken Bridge' in June at SCAF, the last day before it ended. I am glad I did. I think your analysis was very good, in particular the 'gaze'.

ROBERTS: I spent time with Yang Fudong in Shanghai where I conducted an interview. It was after that meeting that I wrote the piece for the *No Snow on the Broken Bridge* exhibition catalogue (2011).

ZU: Were the ideas pretty much your own?

ROBERTS: Yang Fudong is very thoughtful. I drew on what he said and combined that with my own thoughts.

ZU: Do you think Australians are curious about contemporary Chinese art because they are interested in what's going on in China? How would you know if what has been represented through art represents China at the present time?

ROBERTS: Art is visual evidence of an artist's thinking. It is a language of cultural communication. To what extent is the individual or the society the 'author'. That is an interesting question.

Dialoguing with Claire Roberts made me come to realise that for a curator, making a successful exhibition is not the only aim, the significance of the work and its relationship to art history and society more generally are also considerations. Establishing these contexts is not the responsibility of the artist. A hands-on curator, such as Claire, will make such connections and it is perhaps because of this that there is always an exhibition catalogue to accompany her exhibitions.

'I am here all the time, observing it, taking it in and being part of it'

Conversation with Brian Wallace
15 December 2017

Brian Wallace was born in 1957 in Taree, New South Wales. He first travelled to China in 1984 for five weeks as a backpacker. In 1985, he returned to Beijing to study Chinese and has being living and working there since 1986.

From the late 80s, Brian Wallace organised and curated exhibitions for young artist friends in different locations including the Ancient Observatory. In 1991, he opened Red Gate Gallery – the first private contemporary art gallery in China – at the 600-year-old Ming dynasty watchtower in Dongbianmen, Beijing.

In October 2017 Red Gate Gallery moved to 798 Art District. I flew from Sydney in December for the last few conversations for my book. The first of these was with Brian Wallace. He showed me the newly installed exhibition which would be opening the next day. He explained that there are two groups of artists he shows at his gallery: artists who started with him, such as Liu Qinghe, Zhou Jirong, Su Xinping and Guan Wei, and new artists he comes across at art exhibitions, art fairs, graduation shows and via recommendations from artists. He runs the gallery fluidly – some artists move on, others come in.

Brian told me that he is always in his gallery so naturally, our conversation took place at his desk in the back corner of the gallery. This is a shorter version of our dialogue which traversed the ups and downs of the Chinese art scene from the late 1980s to the present, drawing on Wallace's observations and experience.

ZU: This '798, We are Back' exhibition makes me wonder if your intention is to explore political and sociological themes through contemporary Chinese art?

WALLACE: No, not at all.

I am looking for good work which describes what's going on. It doesn't have to be obvious, you know. Those guys grew up in all these changes. They've seen it from the inside – the Chinese side – so they know what's going on. They are the ones commenting on what's going on.

ZU: Could you give me an example? How about the painting on your right? Who was the artist who did the double Tibetan portrait?

WALLACE: That's Sheng Qi's work. The one who cut his finger off.

> *Sheng Qi (b. 1965 Anhui) is one of China's earliest performance artists. He is best known for the act of cutting off the little finger of his left hand as part of the Tiananmen Square democracy protests in June 1989. Exiled from China, Sheng Qi currently makes art in London, continuing to expresses political observations and criticism through his art.*

ZU: Aha! Is he the artist whose work caused the show to be shut down at the Watchtower?

WALLACE: Yes. That was in 2008. His works then were quite different. They were very obviously political. We were already hanging the show, and I hadn't paid that much attention.

ZU: Or perhaps it was not an issue from your perspective.

WALLACE: The mayor of the district came in to have a look at the site – the local government was looking for venues as a means to promote the Olympics – so he came in.

ZU: Ouch, wrong time.

WALLACE: Wrong time, bad luck in a sense. He'd been an old commie so he read it very well. He said we are not going to show this work because I will get the sack. [laughs]

ZU: Ha. What a clever way to persuade you.

WALLACE: Yeah. [giggles] you don't argue with a mayor anyway. Sheng Qi was cool. He knew how far he could go. The invitations had gone out and everyone came to the opening. But we just had spotlights [on the wall in place of the art].

ZU: You still had the opening? I like that! It's absolutely a conceptual work in itself! What did you say at the opening?

WALLACE: [laughs] Oh. I just told them what happened. Everyone understood. Some thought it was funny.

ZU: This 'Brother' of his is much more ambiguous, but the paint drips and his palettes of grey and red give me a sense of anxiety.

WALLACE: Some people are very critical. There are a lot of criticisms in some artists' works.

ZU: What are they commenting on?

WALLACE: Hmm … social change, the bad things about it; people being left out; the environment. We have an artist here who's into Buddhism. People want to explore.

ZU: The spiritual search might reflect their disappointment in the current state of affairs.

WALLACE: Yeah, but their works are beautiful. You don't have to read anything more into it. A lot of young Chinese who come to the gallery ask how they should understand it.

ZU: That is indeed a frequently asked question! What do you say?

WALLACE: There are different ways, I say. Just look the beauty of it, the colour, the content, the composition, maybe. Something they can start to connect with.

ZU: That's probably the best way to introduce them to contemporary art.

As the first commercial gallery in Beijing, Red Gate Gallery had a special 'vantage point', to use your words. You showed some contemporary artists' works even before your gallery was established. Tell me about the changes you have observed since then.

WALLACE: We started at the Watchtower in 1991. We couldn't work there in winter, as there was no heating whatsoever. Then we had a very good offer to set up a gallery at the China World Hotel. Practically speaking, the Watchtower was too far away for people, so we moved there. It was still the only gallery. It was good for me.

ZU: Who were your customers?

WALLACE: Only foreigners. The work was really cheap. An important lithograph of Su Xinping sold for $200.

Being there was good, but the rental was also about to go up. The Bureau of Cultural Relics asked me to go back to the Watchtower. When we went back, they gave us the ground floor as well. We built an office to work there the whole year around.

In 1996 the CourtYard Gallery opened at Donghuamen. The same year, ShanghART opened in Shanghai. There were the two private galleries after us.

Up to the end of the last century, there weren't many opportunities for young Chinese artists because there weren't many galleries.

ZU: How did you find your first bunch of artists?

WALLACE: I was at the Central Academy of Fine Arts.

Brian met some artists during a nine-month bridging course at CAFA studying art history (1990–1). He became their art dealer, exhibiting and selling their work after his gallery opened.

After there being just two or three galleries, [various] artists founded 798 in 2001. Then this place developed. Beijing Tokyo Art Projects opened the first gallery (2002) here. It was mainly foreigners who were interested in art, and the artists of course, but no one else. The local Chinese didn't have the time, money or interest.

ZU: True. Did your gallery make any profit at that time?

WALLACE: Back then? No.

ZU: What made you hang on there? Did you just kept going regardless?

WALLACE: For a long time, I had a part-time job to keep me going. Anyhow, we managed.

> *Throughout our conversation, Brian used 'we' when what he really meant was 'I'. I checked with him to make sure my understanding was correct. Brian said that 'we' is used to include the artists and staff and supporters.*

The role of 798 was something very new because it attracted many galleries. Then came SARS (bird flu), so it was like two steps forward, one step back. In 2004 and 2005 you had the auction houses coming, creating much more interest. You have biennales, art fairs. There's been a lot of structural development.

ZU: Do you see these changes as positive growth?

WALLACE: Yes. It is positive to add to the art scene.

ZU: I am always cautious about things becoming overgrown after the initial growth. Anyway, go on …

WALLACE: And then the word got out about how much fun 798 was and this attracted a whole lot of Chinese for the first time. They were able to come and not be intimidated by galleries whereas their older brothers and sisters or parents would never come – wouldn't even know what the experience was. Now we've seen it has been a good ten years really pushing contemporary Chinese art. You have the art districts in Caochangdi, Songzhuang, Hegezhuang, Beigaocun and Fei Jia Cun.

ZU: Those places are more for the artists to make their work and build their studios.

WALLACE: Yes. There are museums, though.

ZU: Ahmmm … I've been to a few of those museums and the museum staff had no training or interest in art.

WALLACE: Yes, they are from the village.

ZU: I like your insightful observation of contemporary Chinese art. You see it not only as connecting to the art world, but also as relevant to the social structure, political change and much more, don't you?

WALLACE: Yep! I guess I am here all the time, observing it, taking it in and being part of it.

ZU: As the one who opened Beijing's first gallery, 'being part of it' is a very modest description in your case, no?

WALLACE: Well … [smiles] we've been doing this for 26 years. It's, in a way, my life … We have also been doing the artist-in-residency.

ZU: That's the next thing I was going to talk to you about. It is a very important program in many ways. How did you set it up?

WALLACE: It started when Asialink sent one artist to Beijing each year. Those artists got here, moved into a hotel, then looked for a studio, which was hard. By the time they were settled in and getting to work, it was almost time to go home. Each year it was the same. I thought why should they have to go through the same problem each year? As we were the only gallery, we helped them. We found an apartment, back in 2001, when it was still difficult for foreigners to live in local neighbourhoods.

ZU: Yes. There were restrictions. If you hosted a foreigner, you needed to report to the authorities to get permission to stay.

WALLACE: Yes. We found an apartment and worked with Beijing Art Academy. We rented a studio there so the artist had the apartment and a studio. We put the word out, so that other artists could rent the apartment and the studio.

ZU: So, you rented the space first then you sub-let it to artists who came? Were they able to afford it?

WALLACE: You hoped they could.

Brian explained that at the beginning, Asialink sent well established artists such as Lindy Lee and George Gittoes for him to look after. Lindy Lee came back to Red Gate for a residency.

Lindy's 2005 residency continues to contribute to her practice

– something clearly on display at her recent solo appearance at Shanghai's 2017 art fair.

That's how we started. Now we have six studio lofts and two apartments.

ZU: Wow! You've expanded over ... how many years?

WALLACE: 15 years. It became a very important thing for us and the art community to create a space for people to come and work here. Many of them wouldn't have been able to do it by themselves. Since then, we have probably been involved with over a thousand artists from all over the world.

ZU: Do you give them a show?

WALLACE: No. We keep the residency separate from the gallery. We do open studios towards to the end of the month with everyone showing their work. Some of them might be leaving as it's the end of their residency, so it's a farewell. We have a barbeque. We usually have a good crowd come along see the works from eight to ten different artists so it's really a good opportunity for others to see the artists in their studios.

ZU: It promotes the residencies for other artists to come too.

WALLACE: Yes. We didn't think about it in this way, but it turned out to be very good for Red Gate Gallery's reputation. Before, if you were interested in contemporary Chinese art, you thought about Red Gate Gallery. But if you weren't interested in China or contemporary Chinese art, you didn't necessarily know about Red Gate. So now, all these artists who have come to experience China and work here for a while go back and tell all their friends that Red Gate really looked after them, they had a good time, blah, blah. They tell their gallerists, dealers, as well as different circles of people so a much wider group of people now knows about Red Gate Gallery.

ZU: Running the gallery as well as the residency program would be lots of work.

WALLACE: I used to do the program myself. Then we found some people who did the job for free, like a coordinator or a director.

ZU: To obtain experience?

WALLACE: Yes.

Then, in 2010, we had a very good one, Crystal. She was doing well so we were able to get her to build into the budget, a small salary. So she started to be paid. When the next person came, there was a salary.

ZU: So the program progressed gradually.

WALLACE: Now we have a full-time program director and a full-time coordinator. They get quite involved with the artists. They take them to material shops, translate for them, go to the studios, to Songzhuang, take them out to dinner, all sorts of programs within the program. Now we use an English expression, 'Jack of all trades' a person who can do everything – fix the lights, fix the toilet, go to the airport to collect someone – keep all the facilities running. And (be) a housekeeper too – you know Beijing – to keep the dust away.

So they keep the studios neat and in good working order.

ZU: Sounds like the artists are very well taken care of.

WALLACE: Yes, very much so!

It has become a very important program. Now we are working with twelve international organisations, including the Goethe Institute, the Austrian Cultural Forum, Creative New Zealand, Video Brazil and The Red Mansion Foundation (London). Organisations like that sponsor artists to come and work in our program.

And we're also working with other residency programs to take Chinese artists to those programs, and connect their programs with our program.

ZU: What an excellent global exchange!

Another significant show for you and Australia–China relations was the 'Two Generations of Contemporary Chinese Art: Red Gate's 20th Anniversary Exhibition'.

In 2011, Brian organised the 'Two Generations of Contemporary Chinese Art: Red Gate's 20th Anniversary Exhibition'. It was a touring exhibition that showed in Beijing, Shanghai, Sydney Town Hall as part of the City of Sydney Chinese New Year Festival, Manning Regional Art Gallery, Taree (Brian's home town) and the Damien Minton Gallery during Sydney Art Month. Other venues were University of Newcastle Gallery and Melbourne International Fine Art. The final show was at the Linton and Kay Gallery in Perth. In 2012, Brian held a return exhibition at the Red Gate Gallery in Beijing.

> Catherine Croll came to Red Gate Gallery on the Artist-in-Residence program in 2007. In 2009 she took up a role as a director of the artist-in-residence program and was special project director for two years. She assisted with the Australian tour and public programs for the 'Two Generations' show.

WALLACE: Well ... it was a very special show. It was a very special time. When we put it up for our 20th anniversary, we asked the artists who have been with us for very long time – and many of them are well established – to nominate or select a new artist that they really liked, not just a friend. They took the idea quite seriously. So we put them in the show, and you saw both the senior artists, and the new ones.

ZU: They were the new generation.

WALLACE: At the time we didn't have the name – Two Generations – because we really didn't know about the second generation. But when we start to put the show together, it was quite obvious that it was two generations.

ZU: When I saw the exhibition title, I instantly related it to my question at the time about the continuity of the Chinese art. I was curious to see what contemporary Chinese art today is like.

WALLACE: Yep. Quite a few galleries had been looking for the next generation. At that time, you know, it was hard to find the good young ones who were really thinking ... there were a lot of well trained artists, but ... they were not thinking much ...

ZU: I know what you mean. Training doesn't make you a good artist. It takes time to digest what you have learned. From my experience, I had to unlearn what I had learnt in order to create freely.

To many audiences, 'Two Generations' was a retrospective show, but I think that may not have been your only intention. It is not a show about the past, isn't it?

WALLACE: Hmmm ... [pauses, contemplating] [The show] is about twenty years of Red Gate. And the name, 'Two Generations', also suggests that things are moving forward into the future. [a happy tone indicates that Brian is satisfied with this summary]

ZU: Putting such a show together must have cost a lot of money.

WALLACE: It was the Year of Chinese Culture in Australia and we got some support from the Ministry of Culture (China). They covered some of transport costs of the show. There were lots of promotions. The public loved it. The only thing we had to pay was the transport in Australia.

ZU: That's good!

So you came to Beijing with a backpack. Do you ever consider packing your bag and going home?

WALLACE: Not really, no! Because I think what we are doing now will see big changes over the next 25 years. Hopefully it's going to work! We've got this space and the residency program. It's been tough for a few years but getting to grips with the internet platforms and social media, working through these challenge, with good staff, maybe we will get there!

ZU: You will get there! How did you feel about moving out from the Watchtower after 26 years?

WALLACE: I had known for some time it was going to happen, I just didn't know when. We really had a good time there and it was a very important time for contemporary Chinese art. The building itself is so special. But all the sudden we couldn't have this space, so in my mind, I'd already adapted.

At the Watchtower, we had to close at 5 o'clock. Here we can stay open all evening. We can have dinner parties. [laughs] We have our own bathroom for the first time in 25 years. [more laughs]

ZU: Most people would find hard to let it go …

WALLACE: No. I am fine!

Brian Wallace's account demonstrates a genuine two-way network that has opened up between China and Australia. Although Red Gate Gallery went through great challenges as a result of changes that took place – and are still taking place – in China, a deeper meaning has been forged in the mutually supporting relationship between China and Australia through contemporary art.

Art broadens the relationship

Conversation with Geoff Raby
2 March 2017

Dr Geoff Raby (b. 1953) is an Australian economist and diplomat. Between 2007 and 2011, he was the Australian ambassador to China. After serving in government for 27 years, he now works between Australia and China independently.

The first time I met Geoff Raby was through a mutual friend in July 2016 in Sydney. Geoff told me that he collected art and had some works in his Beijing apartment. I mentioned that I was writing about Chinese-Australian artists. 'I know them very well. I can tell you about them,' Geoff offered cheerfully.

On Tuesday, 2 March, I came to the Australian Club in Macquarie Street in Sydney's business district.

ZU: As you are an Australian economist, a diplomat and a public figure, I find your art collection and support for Chinese artists intriguing. It's the reason I sought to have a conversation with you.

RABY: It all started back in 1986 when I was first in Beijing at the Australian Embassy as First Secretary.

ZU: What is the main role of a First Secretary?

RABY: My area was economics. The other First Secretary who did the political work at the time was Kevin Rudd.

ZU: So you were not in the political arena.

RABY: We overlapped. My work wasn't on commercial the side of the relationship. It was economic. The economic side was very close to the political side.

ZU: You mean there's an interconnection between the two.

RABY: Yes. Because economic work is about government policy. You need to understand government policy – both Australia's and China's.

ZU: It seems perhaps that one way to understand China for you was through knowing Chinese artists.

RABY: Perhaps. Those days were fascinating, because China was still very closed. It was very difficult to have a relationship with Chinese people. You couldn't easily meet locals and develop friendships readily. Chinese and foreigners lived quite separately. But artists didn't have a *danwei* (work unit). It was as if they had fallen out of the system. And they were free to meet and mix foreigners because they didn't have to answer to a *danwei*.

ZU: They were free spirits, floating around.

RABY: Exactly. So they could meet foreigners. That's how the *laowai* [foreigners] and artists got to know each other.

ZU: What were the locations for the meetings?

RABY: Sometimes we would meet in their small hutong homes which doubled as a studio but mostly they would come to our parties. They were great days, exciting days! The artists loved our parties. We had more money than they had, of course. And we had lots of beer.

ZU: How did they get into your parties?

RABY: We had to accompany them, one at a time past the security on the entrances. We had to meet them at the gate of the diplomatic residences.

ZU: I see. How did you meet them in the first place?

RABY: You'd met them at someone else's party, or maybe through a cultural event or something, then you'd stay in contact. That's how the relationships developed. And we used our apartments to show their work because they couldn't show anywhere else, as there was no exhibition space. I had a couple of exhibitions in my apartment in 1987 and 88.

I first met Guan Wei at one of those exhibitions at Nicholas Jose's apartment for example. Nicholas was first teaching in Beijing and then was the embassy's cultural counsellor and he did much to build relationships with the local young artists.

ZU: Tell me about Nick.

RABY: Nick is extremely important in the relationship between Chinese contemporary artists and Australia. He introduced many artists who used to hang out at Yuanming Yuan, near the Summer Palace.

ZU: Did you buy their art?

RABY: Yes. The first piece I ever bought was by Ah Xian when he was a painter.

ZU: Aha. You were his first collector. How much was it?

RABY: Look, it was almost nothing. If we say $200, that's probably too much. [laughs]

ZU: Ha ha. $200 was a lot in those days.

RABY: Yes, and we didn't have so much money in those days either.

ZU: How did Chinese art connect with Australian economics? Did it have a role in shaping or reshaping Australian economy?

RABY: Contemporary Chinese art doesn't have any role in that way. The economic relationship between Australia and China is driven by the very powerful complementarity of the two economies.

ZU: In other words, it is misleading to say that art has a role in contributing to economic growth.

RABY: Art has no role in the economic relationship. But it does broaden the overall relationship. And the role of broadening the relationship is helping people to connect.

Visual art is great because it doesn't require language, so it overcomes the language barrier. People can relate deeply and quickly through visual art.

Chinese contemporary art to me is always very important because it is helping to shape changes in China, by changing China – the way Chinese look at themselves and think about themselves. It's part of a journey between two streams: the classical stream and social realist stream. And it's constantly in a state of evolution …

ZU: Do you mean that contemporary Chinese art evolved from realism because of changes that happened in China?

RABY: Exactly.

So, the first thing is communication because of the lack of language barriers. The second thing is understanding how the Chinese look at themselves. And third, I think, it allows people who do not really understand China to develop a contemporary appreciation of how dynamic Chinese society is – how much change is going on, and how creative and innovative China is today. It is, I think, rather important.

ZU: I agree.

RABY: In my embassy, all the walls were covered with Chinese contemporary art when I was ambassador.

ZU: I remember seeing that. I suppose it was exciting for Chinese stepping into a different world. We were so curious.

Did you select the works?

RABY: Yes. They were all Chinese artists who had been to Australia. It had to be an Australian collection because I was the Australian ambassador. That was the connection. The people who came along, the guests, were very important Australian people and they thought the art was interesting. I managed to sell a lot for the artists. I didn't do it for business, of course. I didn't take any money. But I provided the introductions. When these important Australian people saw the art displayed in the embassy, it gave them a better appreciation of the art, and the value of the art. Then I put them in touch, and the artist could do the deals.

ZU: You also collected Chinese contemporary art yourself.

RABY: Yes. People asked me, 'Why do you have this Chinese contemporary art?' I am very attracted to it personally, of course, but I would say, 'I want to have a conversation with you as a foreigner about the creativity of Chinese society.' Because even a decade ago, when I first went to Beijing as Ambassador, people were still thinking that China was only good at imitating things.

ZU: Copying, making replicas.

RABY: Copying, yes, but not being creative.

Because the economy was developing. China's level of development was at the stage where industry was doing a lot of copying – making cheaper copies of things made elsewhere in the world. There was a view among foreigners that there were no new ideas, no creativity. That's a decade ago. But today that has changed fundamentally. People now understand China has its own brands, has its own creative impulses, and I wanted to show people ten years ago, through the art collection at the embassy, or to alert them, to make them understand that China might be in the copying phase of economic growth now, but soon they would be past that. China will soon be creating novel things. It will be changing itself in the world through creativity.

So it is not just that I like it, but I want to show how creative Chinese society is.

ZU: Did you want to influence people's views?

RABY: I just wanted to show people how creative China was. It was a simple message. As a foreigner you don't think the society is creative, but it is inherently creative, and contemporary art demonstrates that creativity better than anything else.

ZU: I like the way you draw attention to the continuity of Chinese art.

Let's take it further and talk about your relationship with Chinese-Australian artists. I believe you have more to do with them than just collecting their work. How many did you have close contact with?

RABY: Absolutely. I had very close contact with about ten or twelve, people like Ah Xian, Guan Wei, Wang Zhiyuan, Xiao Lu, Hu Ming, Shen Shaomin, [Liu] Xiao Xian, Lin Chunyan, Shen Jiawei, Guo Jian … They were part of the group from the mid-80s.

ZU: What do you think of the effect of the Australian environment on these artists? They tried very hard to get out of China, but many of them voluntarily went back.

RABY: That's because the market is too small. There are three things. First thing, it was then (less so now) much more expensive to live here than China. If you live in China, you can get a big studio space in a way you can never do here. Second thing is the cost of materials. Particularly if you are a sculptor, it's possible to have things made much cheaper. Thirdly the market is so much bigger in China. From 2000, or the late 90s, the whole world became aware of Chinese contemporary art.

You see, there is almost no international demand for Australian contemporary art, even modern artists. It's really not an international market. The interesting thing about the emergence of the Chinese contemporary art scene from the second half of the 1990s is it was in a sense international. It began as an internationally recognised genre that New York, London, Paris and Berlin galleries would carry and wanted to buy.

From the moment Chinese contemporary art was born, there was an international market for it. First it was the diplomats and businesspeople in Beijing [who bought their work], but very quickly, galleries around the world started carrying it.

So that's the main reason they left. And China in late 1990s was a much more liberal open society than the one they had left in the late 1980s.

ZU: I see. But from your perspective, as an Australian diplomat and an influential person, didn't you want to do something about this, rather than letting them go?

RABY: No. I don't think in those terms. They are Australians, and they are Chinese. It doesn't matter if they work in China or Australia.

ZU: It seems you have built up your collection heavily leaning towards Chinese artists.

RABY: My collection extends beyond Chinese art. But, nearly everything I buy is from an artist I know. There's a personal relationship first.

ZU: The paintings are the artist's statement. So the work has another layer or meaning beyond the surface or the object.

RABY: Exactly, very much so!

You know, that's the thing. You can see the artists' personality projected into their work, that's what I love. For example Guan Wei, he has a sly, quirky sense of humour. Nearly all his paintings project that.

ZU: Among all the Chinese-Australian artists, he is the most integrated and very inclusive.

RABY: I agree. He is very modest about his achievements and extremely hard working. He is very interested helping out young artists, encouraging them and promoting them.

ZU: It fascinates me that these artists' works became unique because they reflected their experiences in China and Australia. For example, even though I have never met Lin Chunyan, I can recognise differences in his paintings before and after he lived in Australia.

RABY: Yes. He came here as the same time as Guan Wei and stayed till 2005. He was very important. And before he left, he spent about three months with Shen Jiawei in his home, in Bundeena. There he painted his best work, I think. They were beautiful landscapes and very interesting.

> *Geoff searched on his phone and showed me one of Lin's paintings. It depicted a bushfire.*

I relate to it because of the harshness of the Australian landscape. Australian landscape is very tough.

ZU: Where are these paintings?

RABY: I've got some. They are very thick oil works.

ZU: You first met many of these artists in the 80s, then returned as ambassador in 2007. What challenges did you notice that the artists were facing?

RABY: First of all, it was fantastic to come back as an ambassador because all these people were now living in Beijing.

ZU: Their living conditions had improved.

RABY: Oh, yes. Everyone had an income. They used to be terribly poor. But then they started to make good money from their art. In the first five or six years of 2000s, Chinese contemporary art was on fire. The prices were going through the roof. These guys bought great studios, bought houses. As you say, they were prosperous. There was real excitement in the art scene in those years.

ZU: It didn't last very long.

RABY: Yes. The financial crisis came and the art market collapsed. There was also a general sense that the contemporary art scene in China had turned very commercial very quickly when I returned in 2007.

ZU: Did you discover any young artists?

RABY: I've got quite a number of works by young artists. Unfortunately, I don't know them that well, or I don't know them at all. They are much younger than me. I can relate to the work of the artist, but, they don't fall into the circle of my friends.

ZU: Yes, different interests and experiences.

Let's talk about the values. On one hand, there was the financial crisis, on the other hand, there's the need to support artists. How do you balance out these two? Of course, when you collect a work, you think about value.

RABY: Never. I would say I never think of it. Any works I bought, I thought about the work, how I might appreciate it.

ZU: You are very intuitive when you collect.

RABY: Quite right; intuitive and random. If you look at my collection, you will find it idiosyncratic, and very humorous. There are, I think, some themes. I never tried to buy works because I thought they would gain value. I bought the work, maybe 80 per cent, simply unplanned.

ZU: In a way, there is value, but it's not measured in numbers.

RABY: That's true. [laughs]

ZU: There's another point. Being an art collector and an economist, is not unprecedented. It's been done. What is your focus or new method of engaging with artists that means they show you their good work?

RABY: I find when I am in Beijing – usually not for very long periods these days – all I do is hang out with my artist friends, gallery friends, go to exhibitions.

ZU: Really? Hanging out with artists!

RABY: That's my life.

ZU: How fascinating.

RABY: I think sometimes, if I leave Beijing and come back to Australia, I wouldn't have my artist friends, the galleries, the art scene.

ZU: Sounds like you are becoming Chinese.

RABY: I have become an insider in the art scene.

In the course of my conversation with Geoff, it didn't come as a great surprise that art has little or no influence on a world that is viewed through the close intersections between politics and economics. However, art changes people's attitudes from the inside. By means of a deeper understanding of the human condition in China, art offers Westerners a different angle for observation and a new way of thinking. What fascinates me most is the communication between two cultures that has taken place through the prism of contemporary Chinese art.

The roles that 4A played

Conversation with Aaron Seeto
29 December 2017

Aaron Seeto was born in 1978 in Sydney. His maternal and paternal grandparents are Chinese. Aaron is the third son of five brothers. His family lived in Papua New Guinea until the 1980s as this is where his family had settled prior to their arrival in Australia.

Aaron Seeto was the Director of 4A Centre for Contemporary Asian Art (2008–15) and Curatorial Manager, Asian and Pacific Art, Queensland Art Gallery, Gallery of Modern Art, Brisbane, Australia (2015) before becoming the Director of Museum of Modern and Contemporary Art in Nusantara, Indonesia.

I met Aaron in 2008. I was recommended by Dr Lindy Lee to join the Asia Australia Art Centre (Now 4A Centre for Contemporary Asian Art). I observed that Aaron led his small 4A team not only to develop 4A's role in the cultural contribution of Asian migration to Australia but he also made it flourish and develop stronger relationships between Asians and Australians in the context of art and culture. I was privileged to take part in several of their programs.

This dialogue took place during Aaron's holiday to Sydney visiting his family. We grabbed a coffee from Brewtown and walked to Camperdown Memorial Rest Park in Newtown. We met at 9 in the morning but it was already very warm. Cicadas were singing in the heat. I said to him I would like to focus on the time he spent at 4A.

The Asian Australian Artists' Association was an association of artists formed in 1996. Melissa Chiu was the founding director (1999–2001). The mission was to present and promote the work of Asian and Asian-Australian artists.

The association had a gallery called Gallery 4A. There were two spaces on Sussex Street in Chinatown. Then it moved to Liverpool Street, which had two gallery venues. In 2000, 4A moved to its current site in Hay Street. On Melissa Chiu's initiative, Gallery 4A, was renamed the Asia Australia Art Centre. There were committees of artists. When Aaron came on board, they rebranded as 4A Centre for Contemporary Asian Art in 2009.

ZU: What was the Asian Australian Artists' Association like when you first knew about it?

SEETO: I was introduced to 4A when I was a student at the University of Wollongong. I was interested in curating exhibitions and I was interested in Asian artists. At the time, 4A was the only space where contemporary Asian artists were presented.

I was also interested in the Asia–Australia dialogue. The only place that had this conversation was 4A. So actually my first experience where I understood the power of putting one work next to another was actually at a 4A exhibition. Then I decided maybe I could make exhibitions.

ZU: You worked there in 2001. What did you do?

SEETO: My first job was gallery assistant working under Melissa. It was already a very vibrant organisation, very much driven as an independent space. It was experimental. It was … ahmm … not very well funded.

It was a very interesting time, not just for the organisation, but generally for Sydney. This is when a lot of independent spaces were very active and doing interesting work.

ZU: Any shows in particular from your memory?

SEETO: The first exhibition I remember seeing was an exhibition of Min-Woo Bang, the Korean artist. He was making these luscious and dramatic Caravaggio-style painting. Next to it was this painting by Lindy Lee. That was the moment I thought – well, this is a very interesting way to articulate an idea, by putting two artists together. Of course, Lindy was Min-Woo Bang's teacher, so that added another element of collaboration.

This was Min-Woo Bang's 'Self-Portrait in the Age of Appropriation' with Lindy Lee, Gallery 4A, Sydney, 1999. Lindy Lee is a leading Australian artist and a founding member of 4A.

It was also the first time I had seen contemporary Vietnamese art, a kind of politicised art – whether it was about race, identity or politics – which was driven by people's experiences of where they lived.

ZU: I guess you related to it because this kind of experience of reminded you of your parents and your grandparents living in Australia during the white Australia policy.

SEETO: Yes. That really impacted my development as a young person. In a way it motivated what I do.

ZU: What role did 4A play in this situation? I mean the artists were under all sorts of pressures like this.

SEETO: This is not the most important role 4A played, but it did become a place where people came together. You know, older artists were supporting young artists, exactly like Lindy supporting Min-Woo Bang. There were opportunities to bring artists from overseas to be presented here. It was really a place where artists could come together.

Around the same time, the work of the generation of very well-known Chinese-Australian artists began to be presented. They were having an exhibition at Ray [Hughes]'s, Gene [Sherman] was supporting them and Claire [Roberts] had done important exhibitions. This alternate space was a place for further experimentation.

ZU: What happened in the gap between when Melissa left and you started? There was a period of decline.

SEETO: The challenges were really financial. Funding became harder. People didn't fund-raise the way they do now. It was a very different time and what saved the organisation was people's motivation – the people who ran it and the people who were behind it in the community.

Also, the artists who were involved in it didn't want to see this important but small organisation collapse. When I came on board, there was still a lot of goodwill but there just wasn't the organisation or the funding. People understood how important the organisation was, together with the Board, and in particular the then President, Daniel Droga, we developed a plan to galvanise the supporta and rebuild the organisation.

ZU: I want to talk to you about three Chinese artists' solo exhibitions – Guo Jian (2010), Shen Shaomin (2011) and Song Dong (2013). I think their voices were very provocative in the sense that they were pushing boundaries and teasing out political or social problems. The reason I related to them was because I knew the context. I am interested in why you chose them. Is it possible that their work reflected your radical vision?

SEETO: You know what ... first, there was never a desire to do things just to be provocative. All these artists – Guo Jian, Shen Shaomin and Song Dong – are interesting artists and their ideas fascinated me. Their experience and processes tell us a lot about the role of artists in our society, and the role that artists carve out for themselves in changing social and political contexts. There was no real connection between these three artists, only that perhaps I was drawn to their proposals because they were challenging, and they pushed 4A and also myself to think and organise in more ambitious ways.

4A also saw that it had a responsibility to support these artists, to make public their ideas, and to try and have them circulate within the Sydney art world. The reason I wanted to work with Guo Jian was because at that point he hadn't had a solo exhibition for a while that was not in a commercial gallery. So that layer of programming was really about looking at some mid-career artists who could spend some time to make one body of work, with us fund-raising and getting a little bit of money. It was more about the development of the artist, as opposed to political developments. I am glad that others found them provocative, but this was not our motivation. I also hope that people found them generative. But of course, it is sometimes difficult to separate the politics from the work from this period.

> *'Guo Jian: The Cast and the Crew' (2010) is a solo exhibition based his experience of living between the cultures of Australia and China. Guo was born in Guizhou and migrated to Australia in 1992. He is best known for his satirical paintings that, to quote from 4A's description, 'draw upon his training as a poster artist in the People's Liberation Army. His images meld kitsch and the erotic in a display that is both dazzling and frightening, drawing out the latent violence lurking beneath the surface of popular culture. By bringing the absurd side of life into focus, Guo exposes the politics that underpin contemporary society.'*

ZU: That makes sense. They were born into that era.

SEETO: That's right, it's so much part of their work, but that was not the reason we did it.

With Shen Shaomin, his project was ambitious. At that point, it was the biggest thing we had ever done. His ideas were always expensive. But that's one of the things I love about him, that he's constantly trying to think of different ways to engage with people. He's constantly pushing new ideas. I learnt so much from working with him making that exhibition.

ZU: You knew him a lot earlier than that.

SEETO: We actually exhibited as artists together at 4A.

> *This was 'Transplantation', Shen Shaomin, Aaron Seeto and Paula Wong (2001).*

That was one of the great things about 4A – artists could make proposals to the gallery, then the subcommittee would decide to exhibit them or not. Sometimes we would present an exhibition by unknown artists. At that point, in 2001, Shen Shaomin was living in Australia and we exhibited together.

Then he exhibited with [Huangpu] Binghui. She has made a number of very important contributions to the Sydney scene, if not the Australian scene. I think it's very important to recognise the work she did. Her curatorial vision was always ambitious. She was always trying to find some kind of connection, bridge or relationship between Asian artists' works outside Australia and bring them to Australia.

So, by the time Shen Shaomin made the exhibition ('The Day After Tomorrow'), it was actually the third time that Shaomin had exhibited at 4A.

ZU: I see. I think it is very important for both artists and curators to build a long relationship together. How long did it take to prepare for 'The Day After Tomorrow'?

SEETO: There was a lot of planning that went into that exhibition. I remember I went to see him in Beijing. It was about 12 months ahead of time because this exhibition required a lot of funding to make happen. I remember with Shaomin's show, we went through a number of proposals. He was moving backwards and forwards between Beijing and Sydney, so we talked for a while before committing to the exhibition. There were certain things we couldn't do because they were too expensive or they were physically not able to be created. This man has big ideas.

ZU: You were very critical as well. How did Shen Shaomin take it when there were different views?

SEETO: That's also part of the process. That's one of the roles that 4A played. The reason I see 4A as playing a role is that ability to support or to have that dialogue with artists. Making an exhibition is actually having a relationship with the artist – it is hard to make an exhibition with people you don't have a relationship with. So if an artist and curator can't test each other's ideas, and can't say, 'I don't think this would work, I don't think we can afford it, or the building won't stand it,' then you don't have a real relationship. Shen Shaomin is also the one who likes to have that conversation. So I doubt that he would be interested in just having a one-way monologue. He has an incredible mind, he's an incredible artist, and that is exciting.

With Song Dong it was completely different. I had the idea a couple of years earlier to bring 'Waste Not' to Australia. We began talking to other organisations, other funding bodies. Then we entered to a partnership with Carriageworks. Carriageworks presented 'Waste Not'. Song Dong has said it was the only time the entire installation had been presented.

> 'Waste Not', created by Chinese artist Song Dong, consists over 10,000 objects from his mother's house. It reflects a journey of hardship and grief, resulting in a display of personal resilience and ultimately a celebration of life. In 2013, Carriageworks and 4A Centre for Contemporary Asian Art in association presented 'Waste Not' with the Sydney Festival.

ZU: Where did the idea come from?

SEETO: At that point I was interested in looking into ways we could collaborate with other organisations. We knew that a lot of great work was not being presented in Sydney at the time, and that there were also limitations with what the organisation could actually organise, in terms of our physical building, or what we could afford to materialise. I thought that Song Dong's 'Waste Not' really needed to be presented in Australia. It's a work that engages people on a very personal level, and one that makes evident a process of the artist that is based on relationships and family. It is subtle and also profound. It took a couple of years to get everything lined up. Thankfully, Lisa Havilah at Carriageworks wanted to show the work. She and her team are amazing and they were able to present it there, at the same time we presented a survey of works at the gallery in Haymarket. We would never have been able to present a project on this scale by ourselves.

Lisa Havilah is the director of Carriageworks in Sydney and was previously the director of Campbelltown Arts Centre (2005–10).

I wanted to do a survey show of Song Dong because he is a very important artist. His work has a conceptual underpinning that is distinct from Western forms of conceptual art. I thought it was important for Australian audiences to be exposed to his work.

ZU: I see. The cultural environment is so crucial because it provides both the community and the artists with a way of exchanging ideas and enabling communication. I guess opportunities like this are relatively rare because they require a lot of funding.

SEETO: With every single artist with whom we've embarked on for an exhibition, what has struck me has been their generosity. They knew that we were not a rich organisation but they want to help us to make the exhibition.

Actually, very early on there was an important exhibition. It was with Yang Jiechang ('For Emily' 2003). Melissa Chiu had set up the initial conversation when she was director of 4A, before she left for the United States. It took us a couple of years to come up with a concept proposal. We had very little money, but we achieved a really beautiful and compelling exhibition on one of the smallest budgets. Sydney had a great network of studios and through the state government we secured Jiechang a residency in what was then called the 'Gunnery' Studios. We bought Jiechang an airfare, and he arrived with reams of *xuan* paper under his arm, and in about two weeks he made two 8-metre paintings. He mounted the paintings by himself. This exhibition was very important for my development as a curator – it was a visually compelling exhibition, but it also taught me so much about generosity and collaboration.

ZU: I am impressed that you recognised that sincerity. That works both ways, I believe. I also I know that you have put in many hours of your time. Many artists who have worked with you know that too.

SEETO: Well ... you do it because you think they are interesting ideas to pursue

ZU: When you say interesting ideas, were you intentionally thinking about pushing boundaries or breaking rules, making a statement ...?

SEETO: No.

ZU: You did it because it came from your gut …

SEETO: Perhaps. There is a generous spirit that I think is part of the foundation of 4A. Everything is possible.

ZU: I think that also comes from your being an artist yourself.

SEETO: Maybe.

ZU: You do have a great understanding, an empathy with artists.

SEETO: I think I do understand artists. The way I think is different than others.

ZU: Let's expand on the topic of generosity and talk about the Beijing Studio with Shen Shaomin. How did it start?

SEETO: It started from a conversation. Specifically, I was fascinated by his experience in Australia. At that time, I had moved to Enmore and I realised that he and other Chinese artists had lived around that area in the 1990s. I remember Shaomin saying that at this time he had no money, but he was still compelled to make art. He was bemused by suburban 'clean ups', where households leave their rubbish on the sidewalks, and so he felt that he was surrounded by potential art materials lying around for free. He felt that he had no choice but to continue to be an artist. He had to work with what he had. I think that the works which he produced at the time, made from newspaper and from discarded carpet are very important works. It gave me a better understanding of the experience of Chinese artists in Sydney at that time.

That's the point of the [Beijing] studio, really. After Shaomin returned to live in Beijing, he said to me that he knows that there are great and interesting artists in Australia and that they might benefit from the opportunity to experience China. I think he might have been thinking about his own experience earlier in his career in Sydney. It is a very simple project that came about because he is generous with his own possessions. Shaomin has a beautiful and large studio, he has the space and he wanted to share it with other artists. So I did the budget. It wasn't so expensive. All we needed was the airfare. The cost of accommodation was already looked after. Many of the artists who have spent time in Beijing have described how transformational it has been. I am glad that it is still happening.

ZU: 4A is located in Chinatown. Could you talk about its relationship with the Chinese community?

SEETO: Our relationship to the community was extremely important, because we wanted to better understand where we were located. Also, 4A's history is so much a part of this area, the first gallery was located in Sussex and then Liverpool Streets before we moved to Hay Street. I understood that this arts centre we were running was located in a particular part of the city. I really believed that if you wanted to have a wider conversation, you need to understand your ...

ZU: neighbours.

SEETO: Yes. You want to be a good neighbour. You want to develop relationships where you are living and working. So we positioned the organisation as part of the community, not separate from the community. For me, I was actually fascinated by being able to work creatively with a whole range of people outside of the art world.

ZU: Working with local government is very different from working with artists. Were they open to new ideas?

SEETO: Luckily the City of Sydney is very open. We worked with them over an extended period and in a number of different capacities. They supported us through accommodation grants, through project grants, they helped to broker conversations with different constituencies, and this resulted in a range of programs from an annual street cinema, through to exhibitions and grants for artists to do research in the community.

There was a sense of real openness in the City of Sydney. They wanted to see culture as being a part of the community experience, and I also felt that many of the local businesses were striving for similar things.

ZU: What kind of approach did you take when you encountered people from different areas?

SEETO: Because we wanted to see 4A as part of the broader community fabric, it was important for us to participate, and so I sat on the Haymarket Chamber of Commerce, and I was involved with the Chinese New Year Festival and in the development of the public art discussion in Chinatown. The important part of the work of the organisation was to talk, to advocate for artists to different people, and being part of these community activities allowed us to advocate for artists and for contemporary art as part of that broader community spirit.

ZU: So you had to work on different levels to bring about 4A's objectives.

SEETO: It was an important part of my job to speak widely about our activities and this included meetings with local businesses, to talk about ways in which art and culture could be part of the community experience.

ZU: I can see how that would work.

SEETO: I wanted to ensure that artists' voices were in the local area, for local city workers, people living in the city to look at the organisation and be interested and curious about what we were doing. And also to find ways for artists and the community become together through projects. We did it in a number of ways, not necessarily with Chinese artists. I think one of the most important projects was curated by Toby Chapman with the Indonesian collective ruangrupa and the Australian artist Keg de Souza, who created an exhibition and a whole series of events with international students in Haymarket.

ZU: I remember Cinema Alley. It was always very full. The audiences loved it.

SEETO: Cinema Alley was an important starting point, it was an attempt to give 4A some presence on the street. It presented video and film works by important artists, in a street cinema setting, making work visible to many thousands of people. We presented works by artists including Qiu Anxiong, Ming Wong and Chen Chieh-jen. The street cinema reveals something my attitude towards programming – that if you think art is only for a certain group of people, then you will have a very limited engagement. But if you try and open it up and find ways where all kinds of people can come together, then I think you potentially have a much more fascinating conversation.

I really wanted them to build respect in both directions. You know, of course in Chinatown ...

ZU: ... there's a tension in the mindset about tradition and contemporary work isn't there? This is Chinatown we are talking about ...

SEETO: A lot of people don't understand contemporary art. That's fine. It's totally fine. But what I did want them to do was to respect the role artists play and try to incorporate it within the broader community.

ZU: When you came on board, there was one part-time staff member and yourself. But I think you have brought some significant growth.

SEETO: 4A had always been a very small team. But we were able to increase it quite significantly with funding from the City of Sydney, which was great. It did raise the profile of the organisation and it raised the profiles of the artists in the 'Sydney scene'.

ZU: It worked really well! Look at the Yangjiang performance project at the Chinese Garden in Darling Harbour. The drunken calligraphers' performances were so spontaneous.

'Actions for Tomorrow' (2015) was an exhibition by the Yangjiang Group, a collective exhibition by three Chinese artists

who use the medium of calligraphy as a conceptual springboard into a diverse range of installations and performances. The 'Twilight Garden Party' was held at the Chinese Garden of Friendship, Darling Harbour with the audiences becoming participants.

SEETO: It was extraordinary. It was really rewarding and demanding project that was pulled off by a dedicated team.

ZU: I see how fluid 4A has been – starting from being only on the walls of Gallery 4A, it gradually expanded to include society, then evolved within that society.

SEETO: That's as much because the ethos of 4A was kind of like the idea behind the Yangjiang Group – their idea was that artists are everywhere. Everyone can be part of art – it's their philosophy.

ZU: So it comes down to a mutual understanding about contemporary Chinese art – when no one is asking the question because everyone is in it.

SEETO: Yes.

ZU: Many people have been engaged with and involved with 4A at different levels and times. Of the artists I know, for example John Young was the co-founder of 4A back in 1996 and Lindy Lee was the Chair from 2003 to 2005. They were the backbones of 4A as I understand it.

SEETO: Yes, artists are the foundation of the organisation. When you look at those members who were part of the organisation at the beginning, it is a veritable list – My Le Thi,

Emil Goh, Dacchi Dang, Victoria Lobregat, Vicente Butron, Guan Wei. In addition to Lindy, other presidents included Chris Pang, the architect Kiong Lee (2005–08) Daniel Droga (2008–12) and Dick Quan, the collector, and of course many others. I leant a lot from all of them about the challenges and discipline required to run the organisation.

ZU: There's also been a change from a committee of artists to 4A board members.

SEETO: The counsel that a board gives you can be so important. I am not the kind of person who thinks I can do it by myself or that I have all the answers. It's important to seek advice from people who are wiser than you and more experienced. There are a number of people I do this with.

ZU: I remember you said that Edmund Capon's appointment as chairman of the board of 4A in 2014 was a tremendous appointment. It was exciting news.

SEETO: Before Edmund became the Chairman I asked him if we could have regular coffee dates. He is a person I admire and look up to, and whom I thought that I could learn from. And after he retired from the Art Gallery, I asked if we could still have our coffee days. On one of our coffee days, I asked him to come on board. And he said 'Yes'!

I thought the organisation was at a different stage of development. Having somebody like Edmund on the board would allow the organisation to grow and stabilise in different ways. He has decades of experience.

ZU: Absolutely!

> *The sun is climbing higher and the cicadas sang louder and louder, reminding me that our time was up. I asked the last question.*

You have left the 4A Centre for Contemporary Asian Art, but I trust you've retained a keen interest in contemporary Chinese art. As an artist, a curator and museum director, from all these different perspectives, different levels and scales, how do you see contemporary Chinese art in a global sense? Where will it go from here?

SEETO: You know … the world is constantly changing … so, maybe Chinese art will no longer look the way Chinese art is supposed to look.

It was 10 o'clock. The park had filled up with more people. Everyone was in casual clothes, walking in pairs, walking with their dogs. It was holiday time. I thanked Aaron for taking the time to talk with me. I had been waiting to have this face-to-face conversation since April 2017. But neither of us felt that it would be long before we saw see each. With the internet and social media, we will connect with each other in all kind of ways. We got up, said our farewells and moved on to next thing … alas!

'Suddenly difference becomes interesting, and difference become attractive'

Conversation with John Yu
17 January 2018

Dr John Yu AC is a distinguished Australian paediatrician. He was appointed a Member of the Order of Australia in 1989, named Australian of the Year in 1996, and appointed a Companion of the Order of Australia in 2001. He was the Chief Executive Officer of the Royal Alexandra Hospital for Children (now the New Children's Hospital, Westmead) (1995–97).

For many years Dr Yu has chaired and served on diverse institutions related to art and education. He was the Chancellor of the University of New South Wales (2000–05), a member of the trustees of the Art Gallery of NSW (1997–06), a Life Governor of the Gallery, and was appointed the Chairman of VisAsia when it was launched in 2001. He was also the Chair of the Australia–China Council (2000–06).

Dr John Yu was born in Nanjing and came to Sydney with his sister and mother at the age of three when the Japanese invaded China in 1937.

His father was a senior leader in the Kuomingtang (Nationalist) government and went to Taiwan from Chongqing with Chiang Kai-shek in 1949. John only met his father in Taipei after he had become an adult.

John Yu grew up with his mother's family. His maternal grandfather was a Christian who came to Australia in 1867 as a refugee during the gold rush. He started the first Chinese Presbyterian Church in Sydney. His uncle was a doctor. John performed brilliantly at school. He discovered his passion for paediatric care and after starting work at the Royal Alexandra Hospital for Children in 1961, he eventually rose to become Head of Medicine and later chief executive in 1978.

I met Dr Yu in December 2017 when he opened an exhibition at Simon Chan's gallery Art Atrium – an art gallery exhibiting contemporary Australian, Asian and Aboriginal art with a special focus on cross-cultural collaboration and expression as a reflection of multicultural society in a globalised world. Simon introduced me to John as they had known each other for many years. Among his many roles, Simon is the Director of the Board of VisAsia at the Art Gallery of NSW. I briefly talked to John about the book project and asked if he would consider having a conversation with me. He said: 'Yes! Call me in the new year.'

This is a short version of the conversation I had with Dr John Yu in at his home in Mosman on 17 January 2018, focusing on art as a healing process to connect society.

ZU: I would like to go back to 1996, when you were Australian of the Year. I understand that one of your outstanding achievements was integrating art, design and high quality medical care for the benefit of young people. What are your memories of that time?

YU: I was the head of the children's hospital in Camperdown. It was an old hospital, 100 years old. The government offered to rebuild the hospital either on the present site, which would have been really difficult, but the minister raised the issue that there was already another children's hospital in the city, Randwick, and would we think about moving. They offered us a greenfield site at Westmead, which was the old showground, next door to the adult hospital. They said they would build a hospital for us, which would be freestanding and we would be separate from Westmead Hospital.

We agreed to do that. But at that time, hospital architecture was pretty brutal, like concrete bunkers. I thought that was really wrong for a children's hospital. It needed to be much more gentle and welcoming.

ZU: Yes!

YU: So we talked with the minister and the government architect. It was decided that instead of having one architect, there would be four, and each one would build a different part of the hospital so that it didn't look like a one solid block.

ZU: That's a very innovative idea.

YU: The government took one section, and three private architectural firms took the other three parts. They met regularly so it all joined together.

ZU: It has connections but each one is different.

YU: Yes. Part of that was there would be grounds and gardens because I think one of the greatest ways of healing – I guess, letting go and relaxing – is to use nature. Gardens and trees, things like that are really very important. So that was a very important part of the design. It should have big gardens. There was going to be a courtyard. We turned the courtyard into a Chinese garden.

ZU: Wonderful!

YU: In the Chinese garden, there were Ginkgo trees, all Asian trees, a pond with goldfish, and a pagoda from China. It was a gift.

ZU: When was this?

YU: It started from 1990.

The other thing was in the building we wanted it to be almost domestic dimensions. We didn't want it to have a large institutional feel. I am interested in music and art. It has always helped me a lot. It's given me a lot of pleasure and helped me to relax.

ZU: You brought your own experience to this.

YU: Yes. I talked to the architect again. We said we needed art. Two things: one is to humanise the hospital, and secondly just to say to people we care about you, we care about how you feel. We thought that would help people trust us and trust the hospital to look after their children.

ZU: Yes.

YU: That worked well! I talked to people about it. One of the people I talked to was Joanna Capon. She really liked the idea. She came on board, and found all the works of art. Some of works we bought from money people donated, but most of them were donated by the artists. All the big artists at the time gave us things.

Joanna Capon OAM is an art historian, archaeologist, curator and writer. She was a member of the Children's Hospital at

Westmead's board for ten years and has been the honorary art curator at the hospital since 1995. Joanna Capon has had an enormous impact on the healing environment of the hospital by developing a highly successful program of art donation.

ZU: That was very generous of the artists.

YU: In the foyer there was a big painting of Michael Johnson's. It was a very expensive gift.

ZU: How did you display the art in the hospital?

YU: In the public space – the foyer areas, corridors and waiting rooms, but also in the wards. In the end in the wards, we used children's paintings.

ZU: Were the children's paintings done by the patients?

YU: No. We got onto the Department of Education and asked children whether they would do a painting for hospital. Operational Art is still runs throughout New South Wales. They submit them to a judging panel, which selects them, then we have a show, usually in Western Sydney, but the best paintings were hung in Art Gallery of NSW for six weeks. The ones we think are suitable, we frame and put in the hospital in the areas where children were.

And then it became so popular, we had more paintings than we needed, so we gave them to other hospitals. Not only children liked them. We also put them in maternity units because it makes mothers feels better.

ZU: Of course. This was completely new in the 1990s. How did the architects react to your ideas?

YU: They were very supportive. They understood what we were trying to do. But we only chose those architects who understood and wanted to be part of it.

ZU: When VisAsia was established at the Art Gallery of NSW, you were the founding chairman. How did that come about?

YU: I was on the board of trustees. I was the deputy chair. I chaired the acquisitions committee. Edmund [Capon] and I used to talk about Asian art and how we could bring more into the gallery. It was Edmund's idea that we should start a group and he asked me if I'd chair it.

ZU: And you said yes.

YU: Hmm!

ZU: How did you run it?

YU: The main thing about VisAsia – and it wasn't a rule, but we always had in mind – was that we wouldn't actually buy things, but we would support educational activities. We would support exhibitions. Sometimes it is very hard to get sponsorship for Asian exhibitions, so VisAsia would support them. Or we'd support lecture series, visiting scholars, exchange fellowships, things like that.

ZU: Did you give lectures?

YU: Some. The ones I did were usually about Southeast Asian textiles, particularly Indonesian textiles.

ZU: I see. That's a broader sense of Asian art.

YU: Yes. You see my big interests in Southeast Asian art are textiles, ceramics and Buddhist art.

ZU: You donated a lot of textiles to the gallery, didn't you?

YU: There are very few textiles collections other than some Chinese silks, which is crazy because in Southeast Asia, textiles are an integral part of ritual life. I thought it was very important that we started getting textiles into the collection and incorporating them into exhibitions. That's why a large part of my gifts to the Art Gallery were textiles.

ZU: So they are like spiritual gifts in addition to artifacts?

YU: Art becomes the route through which people see different things in non-challenging way.

ZU: It stimulates the mind.

YU: It's not to challenge their religious beliefs or their political beliefs, but hopefully they will be stimulated in an aesthetic sense by the art itself. People will understand that yes, it's different to our art, and the difference is exciting. It's like when you have a night out. A lot of people, particularly younger people, wouldn't think about having a barbeque. They want to have yum-cha, different food from different parts of the world. Suddenly difference becomes interesting, and difference become attractive. And certainly not a challenge. And I think food and art are very strong, effective ways of introducing different cultures.

ZU: It is a wonderful way to influence people's attitude in a subtle way.

YU: I think art also helps young Chinese, young Muslims, to think, 'That's interesting. That's my culture!'

ZU: To rethink their own heritage.

YU: If they feel proud about their culture, and like their culture and the images of their culture, it helps when other people criticise them or make racist remarks. They will feel better about themselves. I always feel strongly the most important thing for a child is to be loved and feel they are wanted. If you are loved and wanted, you can cope with anything. You can cope with people calling you names, you can cope with anything. I think if we can make young immigrant Australians feel good about where they came from, it makes it easier to withstand other criticisms.

ZU: And to get through the hard times.

YU: Yes. That part of art is undervalued. But it's real.

ZU: I just realised that you are a Christian, and yet you have collected so many Buddha statues.

YU: I was brought up as a Christian. I don't like the way the leaders interpret the holy scriptures. In many ways, I find the teachings of the Buddha much more compatible with the way I feel than Christianity.

Buddhism had a really interesting effect on me. It helps me relax. It makes me feel most serene. I think that's something a lot of artists try to achieve.

ZU: I can appreciate that.

YU: There's Christian music I love, but I also find Buddhist chanting very moving. If you feel stressed, it's very relaxing, I think it's about the repetitiveness. The thing is to let go, and not think about things.

ZU: That's a very good lead-in to my next question about East meeting West. You explained it through music. It serves the same purpose whatever different method you use, doesn't it?

YU: Yes.

ZU: What is your perception of Chinese art compared with Australian art? You have a broad collection, from Western paintings to pottery and Buddhist art.

YU: I accept Chinese art without making judgments because I don't see it as different. It's like I like modern furniture and old paintings.

ZU: Hmmm. That's an intriguing comment. What is the connection you are pointing to?

YU: I guess what I am saying is that I like forms that are well crafted and well made. It doesn't matter what material it was made from, and it doesn't matter which country it comes from.

ZU: Of course. The answer is you. You made the connections between all these different things.

YU: I guess it's my aesthetic values, which is not right, not wrong, not better than somebody else. It's just me.

ZU: Absolutely.

YU: I've been to a lot of auctions, very often estate auctions, and when you look through someone else's eyes, you can see why a particular thing's been chosen. You can see why that person loves one thing more than another. It's nothing to do with monetary value.

ZU: Right. The individual creates the differences and the individual makes the art coherent across history to the present, and around different parts of the world.

YU: And they put together what they like, excluding things they don't like.

ZU: It's very biased. Are we allowed to be so subjective? Is there a point in political correctness?

YU: No. I don't like political correctness.

ZU: How about the Australia–China Council during the time you were chairman? That was a political position in a sense.

YU: Well, it was one appointed by the minister. But I have never been strongly political in the usual sense of the world except for standing up for the rights and needs of refugees. Other than that, I had never been involved with Australian politics. What I really wanted to do as chairman of the Australia–China Council was to foster understanding between Chinese and Australians, and support those things I thought and think would result from that, like exchanges and fellowships for young people, artists, creative people, musicians, writers, philosophers and thinkers.

ZU: Your contribution on the Council seems to have provided opportunities to those who needed assistance but were not famous.

YU: I also thought that the chairman of the Australia–China Council should be Chinese.

ZU: Is this still the case?

YU: No. It hasn't been since I left. I was the only Chinese who held the position.

It was important when I was the Chancellor of University of New South Wales that I went to all the overseas graduation ceremonies because I think it is important for Asians, especially from Southeast Asia, to see that being Chinese is no impediment to achieving important things in Australian education.

But as for political correctness, I don't think they should choose someone just because they are Chinese or Filipino. They should choose somebody who can bring something to the position.

ZU: I agree.

What do personal connections have to do with genuine support for the arts?

YU: I think it's not just friendships, but the fact that people share common interests.

ZU: Do you mean there's value in the principle of bringing people together rather than just promoting friendship?

YU: Yes! Friendship alone isn't enough.

Dr Yu spoke quietly throughout our conversation. However, there was a weight in his words. They were meaningful and stayed with me for a long time. He trusted me and spoke openly about other memories not revealed here. He helped me understand the relevance of his generous acts towards other and the world. I come to realise that the most enduring quality I took from him was his altruism. This selflessness, in my view, is one of the deep-rooted essences of Chinese art, philosophy and virtue.

At the close of the conversation, I come to realise that after two years researching, dialoguing, dictating and writing, the point has come to complete the book because it has returned to the beginning.

Acknowledgements

The Tao: Conversations on Chinese Art in Australia is a call to action, inviting readers to participate in a conversation about art and life.

First, my profound thanks go to the people featured in this book. To Ah Xian, Edmund Capon, Jocelyn Chey, Guan Wei, Nicholas Jose, Lin Chunyan, Liu Xiaoxian, Mae Anna Pang, Geoff Raby, Claire Roberts, Aaron Seeto, Shen Shaomin, Gene Sherman, Brian Wallace, Wang Zhiyuan, Xiao Lu and John Yu, I am deeply appreciative. You were generous with your time and even more generous with your stories.

I am very grateful to the individuals who provided me with invaluable research materials for this project. Thank you to Cao Yin, Simon Chan, Chen Jun, Stephen Gilby, Carol Henry, Judith Neilson, Shen Jiawei and Zhao Li.

I would also like to thank the organisations who gave me access to their archives: Art Exhibitions Australia and the Edmund and Joanna Capon Research Library, AGNSW.

My heartfelt thanks go to my editor, Pamela Hewitt. Your empathy meant a lot to me throughout the editing process.

This project would not have been possible without the financial support of the Australia–China Institute for Arts and Culture, Western Sydney University. In particular, I would like to thank Jocelyn Chey and Wang Labao. I would also like to acknowledge the support of Barney Glover, the Vice-Chancellor of Western Sydney University.

Finally, I would like to thank Alice Zhou for your insightful comments on earlier versions of this manuscript and throughout the writing process, Edmund Capon for your thoughtful feedback, and Jocelyn Chey for your unwavering support and advice at all stages of this project.

Tianli Zu

Glossary

This book uses simplified Chinese characters and pinyin for pronunciation wherever applicable except in cases where a name or title is best known in other transliteration systems, for example Tao Te Ching.

A
Ah Xian 阿仙
Ai, Weiwei 艾未未

B
Bada Shanren 八大山人
baihua 白话
Barmé, Geremie (Bai, Jieming) 白杰明
Bei, Dao 北岛
Beida 北大
Beigaocun 北皋村
Beiwai 北外
bian gushi 编故事

C
Caochangdi 草场地
Capon, Edmund 孔爱文
CC Wang 王季迁
Chang, Johnson 张颂仁
Chey, Jocelyn 梅卓琳
Chey, Moon Lin (Hans) 齐梦麟

Chiang Kai-shek 蒋介石

D
Da Guo 大过
danwei 单位
Deng, Xiaoping 邓小平
Ding, Cong 丁聪
Dong, Qichang 董其昌
Dongbei 东北
duilian 对联

E
Erwai 二外

F
Fang, Lijun 方力均
Fei Jia Cun 费家村
Fong, Wen (Fang, Wen) 方闻
Fuzhong 附中

G
gongming 共鸣
Guan, Wei 关伟
Gugong 故宫
Guo, Jian 郭健
guohua 国画

H
Hanzuren 汉族人
Hegezhuang 崔各庄
Hongbinlou 鸿宾楼
Hou, Hanru 侯瀚如
Hu, Ming 呼鸣

hua 画
Huadong Shida 华东师大
Huang, Binhong 黄宾虹
Huang, Miaozi 黄苗子
Huang, Yongyu 黄永玉
Huangpu, Binghui 皇甫秉惠
Huineng 慧能

I
I Ching 易经

J
Jian 蹇
Jingdezhen 景德镇
Jose, Nicholas (Zhou, Si) 周思

K
Kan 坎
Kuncan 髡残
Kuomingtang 国民党

L
lai-lai wang-wang 来来往往
Li, Shan 李山
Li, Xianting 栗宪庭
Ligong Daxue 理工大学
Lin, Chunyan 林春岩
Liu, Wei 刘炜
Liu, Xiaodong 刘小东
Liu, Xiaoxian 刘晓先

M
Mang, Ke 芒克

Menglong shiren 朦胧诗人
Mengzi 孟子
Muxudi 木樨地

P
Palace Museum 故宫

Q
Qianlong 乾隆
Qin Shi Huang 秦始皇
Qinghua 清华
Qiu, Anxiong 邱黯雄

R
Redtory Art District 红专厂
Roberts, Claire 罗清奇

S
shaonian gong 少年宫
Shen, Jiawei 沈嘉蔚
Shen, Shaomin 沈少民
Sheng, Qi 盛奇
Shenxiu 神秀
Sima, Qian 司马迁
Song, Dong 宋东
Songzhuang 宋庄
Su, Dongpo 苏东坡
Su, Xinping 苏新平

T
Tan, Dun 谭盾
Tang, Song 唐宋
Tao 道

Tao Te Ching 道德经
Tiananmen 天安门

W
Wang, Gai 王概
Wang, Guangyi 王广义
Wang, Youshen 王友身
Wang, Yuanqi 王原祁
Wang, Zhiyuan 王智远
Wei, Jingsheng 魏京生
wenrenhua 文人画
Wenwu 文物
Wenwu Ju 文物局
wenyanwen 文言文
Wu, Hong 巫鸿
Wu, Yongqi 吴永琪
Wu, Zuoren 吴作人

X
Xiangxiang 像想
Xiao, Lu 肖鲁
Xiao, Shufang 萧淑芳
Xu, Bangda 徐帮达
Xu, Bing 徐冰
Xu, Zhonglin 许忠陵

Y
Yang, Fudong 杨福东
Yang, Gladys 戴乃迭
Yang, Jiechang 杨诘苍
Yang, Lian 杨炼
Yang, Xianyi 杨宪益
Yang, Xinman 杨新满

Yang, Zhichao 杨志超
Yangjiang 阳江
Yin, Xiuzhen 尹秀珍
Yu, Dafu 郁达夫
Yu, Feng 郁风
Yu, John 余森美
Yu, Youhan 余友涵
Yuanming Yuan 圆明园
yujing 语境

Z
Zhang, Xiaogang 张晓刚
Zhao, Yanchao 赵燕潮
Zhemei 浙美
Zhongguancun 中关村
Zhongyong 中庸
Zhou, Enlai 周恩来
zhuo 拙
zouhoumen 走后门
Zu, Tianli 祖天丽

Index

Note: Page numbers in bold indicate interviewee's chapter.

Abyss, *Kan*, 266-7
Adversity, *Jian*, 196
Ah Xian, ix, 95, 97, 102, 104, 109-10, 123, 125, 142, 145-6, 149, 157-8, 166, **171-90**, 195, 217, 233, 251, 276, 305, 309
Ai, Weiwei, 58, 129-30, 256
Art districts in China
    798 Art District, 228, 287-8, 291-2
    Beigaocun, 293
    Caochangdi, 293
    Fei Jia Cun, 293
    Hegezhuang, 293
    Redtory Art District, 245
    Songzhuang, 233, 293, 296
Art education, 215-22
Art galleries
    Art Atrium, 338
    CourtYard Gallery, 257, 291
    Gallery 4A, 4A Centre for Contemporary Asian Art, x, 31, 245, 254, 317-24, 326-30, 332-3

Hanart, 147-8, 150
Irving Galleries, 110, 122-3, 201
Martin Browne Contemporary, 113
Ray Hughes Gallery, 222-3
Red Gate Gallery, x, 146, 251, 287, 290, 295-8, 300
ShanghART, 291
Sherman Galleries, 117, 125
Vermilion Art, 101
White Rabbit Gallery, 211-2, 215, 225
Art groups in China
    Acheng Printmaking Group, 248
    Yangjiang Group, 329-30
Art organisations
    4A Centre for Contemporary Asian Art, *see* Art galleries, Gallery 4A
    Art Exhibitions Australia, 23
    Asialink, 294

Contemporary Asian Australian Performance, 31
International Cultural Corporation of Australia, 41, 65, 75
Sherman Centre for Culture and Ideas, 120
Sherman Contemporary Art Foundation, SCAF, 130, 256, 271, 277-80, 282

Art schools
Central Academy of Fine Arts, CAFA, 144, 175, 215-6, 218-20, 249, 271, 291
Fine Arts School Affiliated to the Chinese Central Academy of Fine Arts, *Fuzhong*, 201-2, 208, 211-2, 216, 220
National Art Academy, *Zhemei*, 208
Sydney College of the Arts, SCA, 157, 177, 217, 221, 224
Tasmanian School of Art, 103-4, 233-4

ArtExpress, 148
Asia–Pacific Triennial, 178, 271, 276
Australia Council, 22-3, 103, 107-8, 178
Australia–China Council, 9, 12, 30-1, 337, 346-7
Australia–China Institute for Arts and Culture, 9, 31, 33

Australian art, 19, 22, 102, 111, 117, 152, 195, 222, 228, 277, 345
Australian Embassy, viii, 9, 102, 135, 143, 212, 303

Bada Shanren, 40
Baekland, Frederick, 47
baihua, 44
Bang, Min-Woo, 319-20
Barmé, Geremie, 112, 142, 150
Battersby, Jean, 22, 39, 65
Bei Dao, 142
Beijing Foreign Languages Institute, *Beiwai*, 138-9, 142, 146, 351
Biennale of Sydney, 125, 129-30, 245-6, 254
Boyd, Author, 238
Buddhism, Buddha, Buddhist, Zen, 55, 63, 83, 163-5, 181, 184, 290, 343-5
Bureau of Cultural Relics, *Wenwu Ju*, 80, 291
Burgess, Greg, 47
Butron, Vicente, 333

Cahill, James, 39-40, 45, 56
calligraphy, 37, 44, 49-50, 58, 63, 332
Capon, Edmund, v, viii, 3, 24, 37, 40-5, 47-8, 50, 52, 60, **61-91**, 110, 333, 342
Capon, Joanna, 340-1, 349
Carriageworks, 324-5
ceramic, 63, 72, 88, 177, 343
Chairman Mao, *see* Mao, Zedong
Chan, Simon, 338

Chang, Han-fang, 16-7
Chang, Johnson, 147
Chen, Chieh-jen, 330
Chey, Jocelyn, viii, 3, **7-33**
Chey, Moon Lin 'Hans', 15-8
Chiang, Kai-shek, 67, 337
Chinese art exhibitions
 in Australia
 Pre-20th Century
   A Golden Age of China: Qianlong Emperor, 37-9, 58
   Chinese Archaeological Relics, 23-4
   Chinese Paintings of the Ming and Qing Dynasties, 39-48, 53-58
   Dragon Emperor: treasures from the Forbidden City, 37-8, 46, 59
   Lost Buddhas, the, 82-3
   Qin Shi Huang: Terracotta Warriors and Horses, 63-80
   The First Emperor: China's Entombed Warriors, 82-90
   Three Perfections: Poetry, Calligraphy and Painting in Chinese Art, 37
 Post-20th Century
   Actions for Tomorrow, 331-2
   Coming and Going, 271
   Echoes of China: From Behind the Bamboo Curtain, 110, 123
   Go Figure! Contemporary Chinese Portraiture, 256, 271, 277
   In & Out: Contemporary Chinese Art from China and Australia, 177, 217
   Mao Goes Pop: China Post 1989, 108, 135, 148-50
   New Art From China, 149-51
   Orientations: The Emperor's New Clothes, 110, 123, 201
   Post-Mao Product: New Art from China, 273
   The International Art Festival of New Music and Visual Art, 157, 175
   Twelve Contemporary Chinese Artists, 201
   Two Generations of Contemporary Chinese Art, 297-9
Chiu, Melissa, 317-8, 320, 326
Churcher, Betty, 144-5
Cinema Alley, 330
City of Sydney, 297, 329, 331
Clark, John, 112
cloisonné, 173, 179, 181, 187
continuity, viii, x, 32, 150, 263-7, 298, 309
Cramer, Sue, 111
Croll, Catherine, 298
Cultural journals
   Connoisseur, 67
   Cultural Relics Journal, *Wenwu*, 79

Cultural Revolution, 12, 20, 124, 245, 247, 273

Dang, Dacchi, 333
Davies, Suzanne, 177
Deng, Xiaoping, 139
diaspora, 117, 157, 173
Ding, Cong, 13
Dong, Qichang, 39-40, 50-1, 54-7
Droga, Daniel, 320, 333
Dunn, Richard, 177, 217

Edwards, Robert, 23, 40-1, 44-5, 65, 70
Elliott, David, 246, 258
Elliott, Simon, 178
energy, 95, 112, 152, 211, 266-7, 282

Fang, Lijun, 149, 151, 273
FitzGerald, Stephen, 15, 23, 25-6, 28-9, 32, 66
Fong, Wen, 39-40
Fraser, Malcolm, 74
French Cultural Centre, 145

Gang of Four, 21-2, 27-9, 142
Gang of Nine, 139
Gittoes, George, 294
Glover, John, 20
Goh, Emil, 333
Guan, Wei, ix, 95, **99-113**, 123, 125-8, 145, 149, 173, 195, 217, 221, 233, 249, 251, 274-7, 287, 305, 309, 311, 333
Gugong, see Museums/ National galleries, Palace Museum

Guo, Jian, 177, 309, 321-2
Guohua, 229

Hall, Doug, 178
Harris, Jack, 15
Havilah, Lisa, 325
Henry, Carol, 41
Hou, Hanru, 147
Hu, Ming, 309
Huang, Binhong, 271, 282
Huang, Miaozi, 12
Huangpu, Binghui, 217, 323
Huang, Yongyu, 12, 47
Hughes, Ray, 105, 223-4, 320
Hull, David, 233

I Ching, viii, 3-4, 95-7, 136, 195-7, 265-7
identity, 31, 157, 162-3, 173, 319
immortality, 83

Jaivin, Linda, 112, 142
Jiang, Qing, 21
Jingdezhen, 166, 178
Jose, Nicholas, ix, 32, 95, 101-3, 105, 107, 110, 112, 122-4, 127-9, **133-54**, 173, 175, 240, 251, 305
June Fourth, Tiananmen Square Massacre, 95, 106-7, 118, 149, 157, 174, 176, 201, 252

Kuncan, 40
Kuomingtang, 337

lacquer, 173, 179-80, 187
Lee, Kiong, 333
Lee, Lindy, 294, 317, 319, 333

Lee, Mabel, 201
Leslie, Jim, 65
Li, Shan, 150
Li, Xianting, 147-8, 150
Lin, Chunyan, ix, 102, 104, 109, 145-6, 173, 195, **231-41**, 249, 251, 309, 311
Liu, Pin, 108, 110, 128, 221
Liu, Wei, 150
Liu, Xiaodong, 151
Liu, Xiaoxian, ix, 95, 123, 126, **155-69**, 175-6, 276
Lobregat, Victoria, 333
Lockhart, John, 65

Ma, Li, 179
Manchu, 38, 101, 113, 127, 246
Mang, Ke, 146, 249
Mao, Zedong, 25, 42, 86-8, 124, 247, 252, 256
McKenzie, Archibald, 201, 260
Mencius, 14
menglong shiren, 142
Merewether, Charles, 129-30
Minford, John, 142
Ministry of Culture, 20, 28, 104, 144, 299
Moran, Michael, 280
Murphy, Bernice, 102, 105, 107-8, 111, 143
Museums/National galleries
  Art Gallery of NSW, v, viii, 12, 17, 38, 45, 47, 63-4, 80, 82, 91, 102, 125, 130, 149-50, 157, 163, 166, 175, 271, 273, 277, 337-8, 341-2
  Art Gallery of South Australia, 64
  Art Gallery of Western Australia, 38, 64, 144
  Museum of Contemporary Art, 102, 105, 107-8, 129, 143, 146, 148-50
  Nanjing Museum, 51
  National Gallery of Australia, 65, 75, 144, 179, 215, 223
  National Gallery of Victoria, NGV, viii, 37-8, 40, 45-7, 55-6, 59-60, 64, 73-4
  National Portrait Gallery, 178-9, 271, 277, 278-9
  Palace Museum, *Gugong*, 38, 41, 43, 46, 48, 51, 58-9, 63
  Powerhouse Museum, MAAS, 274, 276
  Queensland Art Gallery, and Gallery of Modern Art, 149-51, 178, 215, 224, 240, 271, 276, 317
  Shanghai Museum, 51-3

Naumann, Klaus, 47
Neilson, Judith, 211-2, 223, 225
Nelson, Howard, 69
New Children's Hospital, x, 337-41
Nolan, Sidney, 238

Pang, Chris, 333
Pang, Mae Anna, viii, 3, **35-60**

Paroissien, Leon, 143
Parr, Geoff, 103, 105-7, 144-5, 174
Peking University, *Beida*, 174
performance art, 201-11, 277, 288
photography, 141, 158-9, 161-2, 164, 222
poetry, 37, 44, 139, 190, 259-61, 283
Pop art, 164-5
porcelain, 49, 166-7, 173-9, 276
portrait, 63, 110, 158, 163, 178-9, 186, 210, 240, 245, 256, 271, 288, 319
Preponderance of the Great, *Da Guo*, 96
Preston, Margaret, 141
Princess's Jade Burial Suit, 24
printmaking, 245, 248, 250-1

Qin Shi Huang, ix, 64-6, 69-71, 79-80, 82, 84, 86-7, 89, *see also* Chinese art exhibitions in Australia, First Emperor and Terracotta Warriors
Qinghua, *see* Tsinghua University
Qiu, Anxiong, 330
Quan, Dick, 333

Raby, Geoff, x, 212, 236, 265, **301-14**
Rattel, Suhanya, 178
resonate, *gongming*, 52
Roberts, Claire, x, 32, 123, 136, 149-51, 178, 221, 223, 240, 256, 265, **269-83**

Roberts, Tom, 20
Rowlinson, Eric, 57
Rudd, Kevin, 303
Ryckmans, Pierre, 16-7

Seeds of Fire, 142
Seeto, Aaron, x, 254, 265, **315-34**
self-cultivation, 50, 97
Sharpeville Massacre, 118-9
Shen, Jiawei, 236, 309, 311
Shen, Shaomin, ix, 109-10, 195, **243-61**, 309, 321-4, 327
Sheng, Qi, 288-9
Shenxiu, 55
Sherman, Brian, 122, 277, 279
Sherman, Gene, ix, 95, 109-11, **115-31**, 256, 276-80, 320
Sigg, Uli, 256, 277-8
Sima, Qian, 89-90
Snow, Edgar, 25
Song, Dong, 129, 321, 324-5
spontaneity, spontaneous, v-xiii, 3, 29, 83, 205-6, 331
Su, Dongpo, 164
Su, Xinping, 287, 291
Sullivan, Michael, 47

Taiwan, 32, 48, 123, 135, 147, 337
Tan, Dun, 145
Tang, Song, 110, 149
Tao Te Ching, v, 1, 193, 263
Thi, My Le, 332
Thomas, Bronwyn, 110, 131, 221-2
Thomas, Daniel, 20, 22

Tiananmen Square, 25, 95, 107, 118, 157, 174-5, 288, *see also* June Fourth, Tiananmen Square Massacre
Tsinghua University, 174-5, 233

VisAsia, 337-8, 342

Wallace, Brian, x, 221, 251, 265, **285-300**
Wang, CC, 40, 57
Wang, Gai, 40
Wang, Guangyi, 150
Wang, Youshen, 149, 157, 175
Wang, Yuanqi, 39, 53
Wang, Zhiyuan, ix, 195, 211, **213-30**, 309
Watchtower, 287-8, 290-1, 300, *see also* Red Gate Gallery
Wei, Jingsheng, 142
wenrenhua, 49-50
wenyanwen, 45
Whitlam, Gough, 22, 25, 144
Williams, David, 108, 144-5
Wong, Ming, 330
Woodward, Roger, 175
Wright, Bill, 123, 125
Wu, Hong, 252, 254
Wu, Yongqi, 90
Wu, Zuoren, 47

Xiangxiang, 256
Xiao, Lu, ix, 110, 149, 195, **199-212**, 309
Xiao, Shufang, 47
Xu, Bangda, 47
Xu, Bing, 149, 273
Xu, Zhonglin, 43, 46

Yang, Fudong, 281-3
Yang, Gladys, 13
Yang, Jiechang, 326
Yang, Lian, 146, 249
Yang, Xianyi, 12-3
Yang, Xinman, 69
Yang, Zhichao, 271, 277, 279-80
Yao, Wenyuan, 27
Yin, Xiuzhen, 129
Young, John, 332
Yu, Dafu, 15
Yu, Feng, 13
Yu, John, x, 178-9, 265, **335-48**
Yu, Youhan, 151
Yuanming Yuan, Old Summer Palace, 233, 305
yujing, context, the, 281

Zhang, Xiaogang, 151
Zhao, Yanchao, 233
Zhongguancun, 146
Zhongyong, Doctrine of the Mean, 93
Zhou, Enlai, 11, 27

www.ingramcontent.com/pod-product-compliance
Lightning Source LLC
Chambersburg PA
CBHW071017240526
45469CB00006BD/1949